60.00

D0858181

The Electrified Mind

MARGARET S. MAHLER SERIES

This series of yearly volumes began appearing in 1991 and is based upon the panel discussions presented at the prestigious Annual Margaret Mahler Symposia held in Philadelphia. Each volume consists of three papers and their discussions presented at the most recent Symposium. A thorough introduction and a comprehensive conclusion that pulls all the material together are specially written for the book. Occasionally, one or two papers that were not presented at the meeting but represent the cutting-edge thinking on the topic are also included. While this format and organization gives these books a friendly familiarity, the books' contents vary greatly and are invariably a source of excitement and clinical enthusiasm. Volumes published so far have addressed topics as diverse as hatred and cultural differences in childhood development, extramarital affairs and sibling relationship, mourning and self psychology, and resilience and boundary violations. Among the distinguished psychoanalysts whose work has appeared in this series are Salman Akhtar, Anni Bergman, Harold Blum, Ruth Fischer, Alvin Frank, Dorothy Holmes, Otto Kernberg, Selma Kramer, Peter Neubauer, Henri Parens, Fred Pine, John Munder Ross, and Ernest Wolf, to name a few. The vantage point is always broad-based and includes developmental, clinical, and cultural variables but the end point is consistently an enhancement of the technical armamentarium of the therapist.

BOOKS BASED UPON THE
MARGARET S. MAHLER SYMPOSIA

- *The Trauma of Transgression* (1991)
- *When the Body Speaks* (1992)
- *Mahler and Kohut* (1994)
- *Prevention in Mental Health* (1993)
- *The Birth of Hatred* (1995)
- *The Internal Mother* (1995)
- *Intimacy and Infidelity* (1996)
- *The Seasons of Life* (1997)
- *The Colors of Childhood* (1998)
- *Thicker Than Blood* (1999)
- *Does God Help?* (2000)
- *Three Faces of Mourning* (2001)
- *Real and Imaginary Fathers* (2004)
- *The Language of Emotions* (2005)
- *Interpersonal Boundaries* (2006)
- *Listening to Others* (2007)
- *The Unbroken Soul* (2008)
- *Lying, Cheating, and Carrying On* (2009)
- *The Would of Mortality* (2010)
- *The Electrified Mind* (2011)

The Electrified Mind

Development, Psychopathology, and Treatment in the Era of Cell Phones and the Internet

Edited by
Salman Akhtar, MD

JASON ARONSON
Lanham • Boulder • New York • Toronto • Plymouth, UK

Published by Jason Aronson
A division of Rowman & Littlefield Publishers, Inc.
A wholly owned subsidiary of The Rowman & Littlefield Publishing Group, Inc.
4501 Forbes Boulevard, Suite 200, Lanham, Maryland 20706
http://www.rowmanlittlefield.com

Estover Road, Plymouth PL6 7PY, United Kingdom

British Library Cataloguing in Publication Information Available

Library of Congress Cataloging-in-Publication Data

The electrified mind : development, psychopathology, and treatment in the era of cell
phones and the internet / Salman Akhtar.
    p. cm. — (Margaret S. Mahler series)
 Includes bibliographical references and index.
 ISBN 978-0-7657-0804-5 (cloth : alk. paper) — ISBN 978-0-7657-0806-9
(electronic)
 1. Internet—Psychological aspects. 2. Communication—Technological innovations.
3. Communication—Psychological aspects. 4. Cyberspace—Psychological aspects.
I. Akhtar, Salman, 1946 July 31-
 BF637.C45E44 2010
 155.9—dc22   201132282

Printed in the United States of America

To

the memory of

HELEN MEYERS

(1925–2010)

with respect and affection

Contents

Acknowledgments ix

1 The Cell Phone-Internet Lexicon: Overview and Implications 1
Salman Akhtar and Kavita I. Nayar

2 Minds on Media: Implications for Young People in the Internet Age 21
Joanne Cantor

3 The Epidemic of Information: Pros and Cons 35
John L. Frank

4 Cyberspace, Transitional Space, and Adolescent Development 43
Christine C. Kieffer

5 Cyberplay: The Pros and Cons of a "Macrosphere" 63
Monisha C. Akhtar

6 Reality in Cyberspace: Patients' Use of the Internet and
Ordinary Everyday Psychosis 73
Patricia L. Gibbs

7 Preoedipal Paradise in the World of the Web 89
Frederick Fisher

8 The Electronic Couch: Some Observations about Skype Treatment 99
Ralph Fishkin and Lana Fishkin

9 Separation, Sex, Superego, and Skype 113
Jerome S. Blackman

10 The Multiple Meanings of the Electrified Mind 129
Ann G. Smolen

References 141

Contents

About the Editor and Contributors   153

Index   155

Acknowledgments

The chapters in this book, with the exception of chapters 1, 8, 9, and 10, were originally presented at the 41st Annual Margaret S. Mahler Symposium on Child Development held on April 10, 2010. First and foremost, therefore, I wish to express my gratitude to the Department of Psychiatry of Jefferson Medical College, the main sponsor of this event. I am especially indebted to Drs. Michael Vergare, chairman of the Department of Psychiatry and Human Behavior of Jefferson Medical College, Bernard Friedberg, president of the Psychoanalytic Foundation of the Psychoanalytic Center of Philadelphia, and William Singletary, president of the Margaret S. Mahler Foundation, for their kind support of the symposium. Finally, I wish to acknowledge my sincere appreciation of Ms. Jan Wright, for her efficient organization of the symposium and for her skillful assistance in the preparation of the manuscript of this book.

Chapter One

The Cell Phone-Internet Lexicon: Overview and Implications

Salman Akhtar and Kavita I. Nayar

Among the scientific inventions of the late twentieth century none has had greater impact upon the daily life of human beings than the Internet. It has made knowledge—from the news of the day to the minutest details of science and humanities—available to anyone who has a moment to get in front of a luminescent screen and press a few keyboard buttons. Besides thus laying down the external world of facts and figures at our feet, the Internet has also provided the opportunity for traffic in the opposite direction. We now have the possibility of pouring out the contents of our inner worlds (for example, thoughts, opinions, fantasies, daydreams) into the bottomless container of cyberspace. This gives us a sense of greater personal freedom. And, finally, there is e-mail. Linking businesses and individuals across cities, states, nations, and continents in a matter of seconds, this magic carpet of communication can help establish needed links and reduce loneliness, besides, of course, expediting matters of more tangible sort.

These three facets of the Internet's impact (bringing external reality closer, permitting freer expression to the internal world, and enhancing communication) have negative consequences as well. Not all that passes off as "facts" on the net is reliable. Self-revelation can become habitual and lead to fading of real relationships. And, the "merger between communication and technology" (Dini, 2009) can lead to diminished empathy with the recipient of one's scribblings.

While such positive and negative aspects of the Internet are becoming better known and are addressed in this book, the emergence of an entirely new vocabulary involving Internet use as well as the dependence upon cell phones is less often commented upon. The fact is that a large number of terms, phrases, slang, acronyms, and colloquialisms have cropped up in this realm. Hungry customers of the cyberworld are constantly munching on this electronic word salad. This, as might be expected, has psychological consequences and might even have an impact upon the conduct of psychotherapy and psychoanalysis. In this context, the designation of psychoanalysis by Freud's (1893) patient, Anna O., as "talking cure" and its recent modification into "listening cure" (Akhtar, 2007; Nosek, 2009) comes to mind. Regardless of which of these two one prefers, the fact is that psychoanalysis is deeply engaged with language and this involvement has a wide range. The interface between language and psychoanalysis includes free association, transposition of words in parapraxes, obscene words' capacity to mobilize anxiety, representation of things by words and vice versa, the poetics of interpretation, the dilemma of bilingual analytic dyads, and, indeed, the very structuring of the system unconscious (Shapiro, 1979; Amati-Mehler et al., 1993).

Before going into how the newly emergent "cyber-language" impacts upon the areas mentioned above, we would offer a collection of the words that figure prominent in this lexical conundrum.

A NEW LANGUAGE

@: with the advent of the Internet, the @ symbol (pronounced "at") has become commonplace, used in web and e-mail addresses and more recently on Twitter (see entry below) and Facebook (see entry below) to link another user to a "tweet" (see entry below) or status update.

Address: see "web address."

App: see "application."

Apple: see "Apple Inc."

Apple Inc.: an American multinational corporation that designs and markets consumer electronics, computer software, and personal computers. The company's best-known hardware products include Macintosh computers, the iPod, the iPhone, and the iPad. Established on April 1, 1976, in Cupertino, California, and incorporated January 3, 1977, the company was previously named "Apple Computer."

Application: also referred to as a program or "software" (see entry below), an application is essentially a programmed set of directions that guides a computer's "hardware" (see entry below) to accomplish specific tasks like word processing, photo editing, creating presentations, etc. Using the tagline "there's an app for that," iPhone commercials have popularized the use of "app," or the abbreviation of application, in lieu of the full word.

Application software: see "software."

ARPANet: see "Internet."

Avatar: originally a Sanskrit word meaning "descent of a deity from heaven," avatar has been adopted by the gaming community as a reference to a person's video game character, who—like its ancestral namesake—exhibits superhuman qualities.

Bandwidth: a measurement of how much information can pass through a channel. Higher bandwidths facilitate the flow of more information.

BBM: see "BlackBerry Message."

BBMing: the colloquial way of saying "BlackBerry messaging" (see entry below). A BlackBerry user is often seen feverishly "BBMing."

BlackBerry is a line of mobile e-mail and "smartphone" (see entry below) devices developed by Canadian company Research In Motion (RIM). While including typical smartphone applications (address book, calendar, to-do lists, etc., as well as telephone capabilities on newer models), the BlackBerry is primarily known for its ability to send and receive Internet e-mail wherever it can access a mobile network of certain cellular phone carriers.

BlackBerry Message: is the instant messaging service offered by the BlackBerry smartphone that allows BlackBerry users from different wireless networks to engage in one-on-one or group conversations. No other smartphone offers this chat room function.

BlackBerry Messaging: sending instant messages from a BlackBerry device.

Block: The virtual equivalent of a restraining order, to "block" someone means to create a virtual barrier from such a person to discontinue contact.

Blog: see "weblog."

Blogger: someone who posts content to a "weblog" (see entry below) or an e-journal.

Blogging: posting contents on a "weblog" (see entry below) or an e-journal.

Blogosphere: with reference to the biosphere, the "blogosphere" symbolizes the virtual world created by the blogging community, which is often regarded as a unified voice in comparison to traditional media.

Bookmark: a tool available on a web "browser" (see entry below) that stores links to favorite websites for quick and easy access.

Boot: a means to start a computer, for example, "my computer is taking so long to boot."

Boot up: see "boot."

BRB: an acronym meaning "be right back" that is used to indicate leaving a computer unattended for a period of time, thus explaining a pause in an instant messaging conversation.

Browser: a conduit for accessing the Internet, which reads and translates web code into a user-friendly language. Internet Explorer, Mozilla, Fire-fox, Safari, and Google Chrome are all types of a "browser" or "web browser."

BTW: an acronym for "by the way" used in instant messages, text messages, and e-mail messages.

Cell phone: a wireless, portable telephone; also called "mobile phone" or simply "mobile" in certain other countries.

Chat: online conversation that can take place over instant message or in a chat room.

Chat room: the virtual shared space where people can go to chat with other users interested in the same topic.

Chat roulette: launched in 2009, "chat roulette" is a social networking website where users video chat—by using web cams and instant messaging—with a revolving group of users. Like the casino game, the virtual wheel spins at the request of a user to reveal a new chat partner.

Click: the onomatopoeia for the sound made by a computer mouse in action. A "left-click" (pressing the mouse's top left corner with the index finger) navigates away from the current screen by activating a program, opening a file, or accessing a link. The related action is to "point-and-click," or drag the cursor to hover over a desired program, file, or link and left-click to open. A "right-click" produces a tool bar with varying options for what the arrow is currently hovering over. A "double-click" is intended to view content stored in a computer; one should hover the arrow over the appropriate icon and "double-click" the left-side of a computer's mouse.

Command-line interface: a mechanism for interacting with a computer operating system or software by typing commands to perform specific tasks. This text-only interface contrasts with the use of a mouse pointer with a graphical user interface to click on options, or menus to select options.

Communities: Internet "communities" are open forum discussion boards through which users create virtual communities based on shared interest, background, or sometimes dilemma. Many people dealing with the loss of a loved one, the strife of divorce, or a personal illness are active in online communities to help them cope.

Computer: a programmable machine that receives input, stores and manipulates data, and provides output in a useful format. Simple computers are small enough to fit into small pocket devices, and can be powered by a small battery. "Personal computers" in their various forms are what most people think of as "computers." However, the embedded computersfound in many devices from MP3 players to fighter aircraft and from toys to industrial robots are the most numerous.

Computer virus: see "virus."

Connectivity: refers to the ability to access the Internet. It can also refer to the speed of an Internet connection.

Cookies: hidden files sent from the Internet and stored to a computer that track an individual's activity. While convenient in some cases, such as maintaining an online shopping cart and saving login information, cookies are not always as appealing as they sound and can be regarded as breaches of privacy.

Copy: to create a replica of the selected folder, file, or part of a file such as a line of text that can be "pasted" to another location.

CrackBerry: a nickname for the BlackBerry smartphone that compares it to an addiction and alludes to the obsessive behavior of its users.

Cursor: comprises many things: a part of any of several scientific instruments that moves back and forth to indicate a position, a moving icon or other representation of the position of the pointing device on a computer, or an indicator, often a blinking line or bar, indicating where the next insertion or other edit will take place.

Cut: to remove the selected folder, file, or part of a file such as a line of text from its original location.

Cybersitter: a virtual babysitter, "cyber sitter" is a type of filtering software that "watches over" children as they peruse the Internet by censoring what content is available to them.

Cyberbullying: popular among teenagers, it involves verbally attacking, threatening, or distributing evidence of an attack on someone online, most often through the use of social media channels such as Facebook, Myspace, or YouTube (see entries on all three below).

Cyberchondriac: someone who persistently uses online medical information to look up imagined symptoms and diagnose the problem.

Cybercide: virtual homicide that can refer to the death of an avatar in a video game or the demise of a cyberspace persona.

Cybersex: as virtual sex, "cybersex" involves the use of language to simulate the physical act. Like traditional courtship, cybersex often begins in a public chat room as flirtatious banter, then continues in a private chat via instant message, which can escalate the conversation into textual foreplay and more.

Cyberspace: a colloquialism used to describe the virtual environment of the Internet.

Cyberstalking: virtually stalking someone by using web tools such as Google search and Facebook to gather information about the person. While physically stalking someone is condemned, cyberstalking is an accepted albeit guilty pleasure for many.

Dashboard: a personalized page of "widgets" and "RSS feeds" (see entries below) that a user can create on certain websites or for certain applications.

Desktop: what is visible on a computer screen when all programs are minimized or closed, and displays icons with shortcuts to frequently used programs. Also the corresponding term on a laptop, describing an immobile computer workstation that sits on a desk or table.

Digital audio player: see "MP3 player."

Domain name: the identifying element of a website's web address. For example, CNN's web address is http://www.cnn.com, and its domain name is "cnn."

Double click: see "click."

Download: to store or save a file or application to one's computer or cell phone. The opposite of "download" is "upload" (see entry below).

Ego-surfer: someone who searches his or her own name on the Internet to see what information is available online and how he or she is presented to the public.

E-mail: the customary term for electronic mail that one receives via the Internet. A conversation that develops over multiple e-mails is known as an "e-mail thread."

E-mail blast: like an explosion, an "e-mail blast" sends the same e-mail into the inboxes of many individuals instantaneously with a single click of the send button.

E-mail thread: see "e-mail."

Emoticons: facial expressions created by letters, numbers, and punctuation symbols, for example, a smile is represented as :-), surprise is represented as :-o

EOM: appearing after a message in the subject line of an e-mail, this acronym for "End of Message" signifies to the recipient that they will read the sender's message in its entirety without opening the e-mail.

Facebook: began in 2004 as a virtual interactive directory of people that was only available to students at a select group of universities. Now open to anyone, Facebook has more than 400 million users and can be displayed in seventy-four languages. Facebook allows users to create an online profile; connect and communicate with friends, family, and colleagues; share media such as photos, videos, and links; and find new people to add to their networks. "Fan," "like," "news feed," and "poke" are all terms that originated on Facebook.

Fan: used on Facebook to describe someone who self-selects to be in a group of people who "like" a person, place, or thing; "fan" is also used as a verb meaning "endorse" rather than "wave air to produce a cooling effect," for example, "'fan us' on Facebook to support our cause."

Floppy: see "floppy disc."

Floppy disc: pre-dating the hard disc, zip disc, and compact disc, the "floppy disc" is one of the first methods used to transport data from one computer to another, and was simply known as a "floppy" due to the object's flexibility.

Follow: see "Twitter."

Followers: see "Twitter."

Forward: to send an e-mail one has received to another person is to "forward" that e-mail.

Friend: a "friend" on Facebook can range from a relative, a best friend, an old college buddy, and a co-worker to an ex-boyfriend, the mailman, a stranger you shared cocktails with waiting for your flight to board, or even a total enemy. "Friending" someone, or sending a request to be added to his or her friend list, is considered much less intrusive than asking for a phone number or e-mail. If you want to keep tabs on them or keep in touch with them, you "friend" them.

Friending: see "friend."

Gaming: short for "video gaming," describes the community, culture, and multi-billion dollar industry that has developed around video games, or interactive, virtual reality media.

G-chatting: see "g-mail."

G-mail: a "Google" (see entry below) venture which offers instant messaging capabilities, is also commonly used as a verb, for example, "g-mailing" or "g-chatting."

G-mailing: see "g-mail."

GNOC: an acronym for "Get Naked On Camera," GNOC is used in an online conversation to request someone use his or her "webcam" to record the act of undressing. As a topic broached online, many parenting websites warn against its popular use by minors.

Google: twelve-year-old company most widely known for its comprehensive search engine. Also offering email, photosharing, and mapping services among others, "Google" has become one of the most well-branded Internet companies today, and is even used as a verb to describe the act of searching for or looking up something or someone, for example, "if you don't know, just 'google' it." "I didn't know who shot John F. Kennedy, so I 'googled' it." "I spent an hour 'googling' the best vacation destinations, and I realize I can't afford any of them!"

Google stalking: involves extensive "google" (see entry above) research on someone, a public figure, an acquaintance, or even a complete stranger, that would knowingly be deemed obsessive and/or inappropriate in "real life."

Googled: see "Google."

Googling: see "Google."

Graphical user interface: type of computer user item that allows one to interact with programs in more ways than typing such as computers; hand-held devicessuch as MP3 players, portable media players, or gaming devices; household appliances and office equipment with images rather than text commands.

Handheld device: see "mobile device."

Handle: a person's online moniker, often used as a domain name for his or her personal website or as a username in a chat room or on a discussion board. With his heavily followed website, www.perezhilton.com, popular celebrity blogger Perez Hilton exemplifies the use of a "handle" to create an Internet persona separate from reality.

Hard disc drive: see "hard drive."

Hard drive: the large piece of "hardware" (see entry below) on a computer that stores the data necessary to run "software" (see entry below).

Hardware: encompasses the electronic devices and equipment of a computer. Unlike "software" (see entry below), "hardware" refers collectively to the tangible elements that make a computer system run.

Helicopter parent: contemporary term for a parent who pays extremely close attention to his or her child's or children's experiences and problems, especially at educational institutions. Helicopter parents are so named because, like helicopters, they hover closely overhead, rarely out of reach, whether their children need them or not. They also closely watch their children's use of the Internet.

Homepage: the starting page, or welcome page, of a website. Most websites feature a brand logo on each page of the website, which leads the user back to the "homepage" when clicked.

Hot spot: a public place that offers wireless access through a "Wi-Fi" (see entry below) network.

HTML: short for "HyperText Markup Language," it is the code that underlies the way a web browser displays the text and pictures on a web page.

Hyperlink: clickable text or photos called "links" that direct the user to different sections of a web page, another web page on the same website, or a different website altogether. "Hyperlink" is also sometimes called "hypertext."

Hypermedia: describes the "hyperlink" to multimedia files such as music or video.

Hypertext: see "hyperlink."

HyperText Markup Language: see "HTML."

Icon: a visual indicator for a computer program located on a computer desktop or "web browser" (see entry below).

IMHO: shorthand for "in my honest opinion."

IMing: see "instant messaging."

Instant messaging: chatting online and in real time with each other.

Interactive media: two-way communication systems like the Internet and video games are considered "interactive media" because the user must engage with the medium to produce an effect. Whereas a television show will continue without direction, the former require a user to create the experience.

Interface: much like face makeup, the "interface" of a computer or program is the aesthetically pleasing layer of an application that shields the user from the inner workings of a program and facilitates interaction. Frequent changes to Facebook's interface have confused, and even angered, millions of users.

Internet: a complex communication network linking computers to each other that makes instantaneous data transfer and communication possible. Though former Vice President Al Gore famously announced himself as the inventor of the "net" in the 1990s, it had actually existed for many years as the ARPANet (Advanced Research Projects Agency Network), created by a research team of the Massachusetts Institute of Technology and the Defense Advanced Research Projects Agency (DARPA) of the Department of Defense, and was the predecessor of the contemporary Internet.

Internet troll: nickname for a person who purposefully leaves offensive and gratuitous comments on Internet discussion boards, blogs, and chat rooms to incite adverse reactions from others.

Intranet: as opposed to the public "Internet," it refers to a private online portal that is restricted in access to a specific network of people. Most businesses and schools have an "Intranet," where employees and students can access applications and documents unavailable to the public.

iPad: the latest creation by Apple (see entry above), it is a portable web browser and media player. A larger version of the "iPod" (see entry below), the "iPad" can operate the same applications and offers many more specifically designed for its large touch screen.

iPhone: a "mobile device" and "smartphone" (see entries below) produced by Apple (see entry above) through which a user can make phone calls, check e-mail, listen to and download music, watch videos, and add applications with even more creative features.

iPod: a portable "MP3 player" (see entry below) and data storage device produced by Apple (see entry above) that has dominated the portable music player market since its inception.

Keyboard: the piece of hardware comprised of buttons for letters, numbers, characters, and commands that a user manipulates to input information to a computer; also called "keypad."

Keypad: see "keyboard."

Landing page: see "homepage."

Laptop: named for its ability to sit on a lap, it is a portable computer system that has undergone several incarnations which have made it increasingly slimmer and easier to transport.

Left click: see "click."

Like: Facebook (see entry above) users click on buttons or highlighted text that say "like" to give positive feedback to a post such as a status update, link, or photo. Replacing the former Facebook term "Fan" (see entry above), "Like" is also used to denote association to a Facebook page.

Link: see "hyperlink."

Listserv: a categorized roster of e-mail addresses that a sender can select as the recipient of an e-mail and all list members will receive the e-mail simultaneously.

Live chat: common term used to describe an instant messaging "widget" (see entry below) used on commercial websites to provide immediate and convenient customer support.

LMAO: acronym for "laughing my ass off."

LOL: "laugh out loud," a common acronym used in online and text message conversation.

Lurker: someone who frequents chat rooms and discussion boards but rarely participates in the conversation.

Mac: see "Macintosh."

Macintosh: a series of several lines of personal computers designed, developed, and marketed by Apple Inc.The first Macintosh was introduced on January 24, 1984. It was the first commercially successful personal computer to feature a mouse and a graphical user interface rather than a command-line interface.

Malicious software: see "malware."

Malware: short for "malicious software"; refers to the software designed to infiltrate a computer system without the owner's informed consent. The expression is a general term used by computer professionals to mean a variety of forms of hostile, intrusive, or annoying software. The term "computer virus" is sometimes used as a catch-all phrase to include all types of malware, including true viruses.

Mobile: see "cell phone."

Mobile device: any portable communication system such as a "laptop," "cell phone," "smartphone," and "PDA" (see separate entries).

Mobile phone: see "cell phone."

Modem: computer hardware that connects a computer to the Internet by using a telephone connection to transmit information.

Monitor: computer hardware that displays computer activity; also known as the computer "screen."

Mouse: external device that connects to the computer and controls the "cursor" on a computer "screen."

Mouse potato: similar to its namesake the "couch potato," a "mouse potato" is someone who spends a great deal of time surfing the Internet in a passive, or lazy, manner.

MP3 player: a consumer electronic device that has the primary function of storing, organizing, and playing audio files. A "digital audio player" is usually referred to as an "MP3 player." Common features of all MP3 players are a memory storage device, such as flash memory or a miniature hard disk drive, an embedded processor, and an audio coded microchip to convert the compressed file into an analogue sound signal. In October 2001, Apple Computer unveiled the first generation iPod, a five gigabyte hard-drive based DAP. In July 2002, Apple introduced the second generation update to the iPod. It was compatible with Windows computers through Musicmatch Jukebox. The iPod series, which grew to include flash memory-based players, has become the market leader in DAPs.

MySpace: a social networking site where users can showcase their personality by customizing their personal profiles with personalized "skins," soundtracks, photos, videos, diaries, and friend lists. Many aspiring musicians have successfully used their MySpace accounts to distribute original music online, generate buzz, grow an audience, and promote themselves.

Navigate: now refers more often to the process of browsing the cyber terrain than crossing bodies of water or discovering new land.

Net: see "Internet."

Net lingo: in addition to referring to online jargon, "net lingo" also pertains to new words introduced as a result of technology like new business and marketing expressions that have developed such as website "stickiness," "coolhunting," "conversion rate," and "webinar."

Netiquette: derived from the words "net" and "etiquette," netiquette refers to the unofficial set of rules regarding proper decorum in the online environment. An example of "netiquette" is to reply to an e-mail within a few days of receiving it.

Netspeak: terminology that has developed for use on, and in relation to, the Internet and mobile devices, including acronyms, emoticons, technical terms, and colloquialisms.

News feed: as displayed on Facebook's homepage, it is an automatically updated catalog personalized to each user that highlights his or her friends' recent Facebook activity such as status updates, new photo albums, comments, wall posts, and other profile updates.

NSFW: short for the phrase "not safe for work," a warning to the user before viewing mature content that would be inappropriate in certain settings.

Offline: the state of not being online, or connected to the Internet. A computer is offline when it loses connectivity.

OMG: meaning "oh my God," is used to concisely express surprise.

Online: refers to being connected to the Internet, for example, "I lost track of time and spent all evening online"; or to being found on the Internet, "Many students use online research, but fail to check its credibility."

Operating system: a computer's most significant "software," controlling all applications and ensuring the proper functioning of its hardware. Windows and Mac are two widely recognized examples of operating systems.

P2P: see "peer-to-peer networking."

Palm Pilot: see PDA.

Password: a private word or combination of letters and/or numbers that is known only by the Internet user and helps him or her access e-mails and other services.

Paste: relocation of a folder, file, or part of a file such as a line of text after it is cut or copied from the original location.

PC: refers to "personal computer."

PDA: the predecessor to the smartphone, a "PDA" or Personal Digital Assistant is a handheld mobile device that contains electronic versions of personal organization staples such as a calendar, address book, and memo pad. The "Palm Pilot" is an example of a PDA.

PDF: see "portable document format."

Peer-to-peer networking: actually computer-to-computer networking, where computers and the users controlling them can share files with each other without the administrative oversight of a server. Limewire, Kazaa, and Bearshare are all examples of P2P networks well known for music and video sharing.

Phishing: used by scam artists, "phishing" is an identity theft strategy that involves sending a fraudulent e-mail from a credible source to people with the intention of collecting personal and financial information like birthday, social security number, credit card number, and bank account number.

Podcast: a free audio file that can be downloaded to a computer, and then uploaded to a digital music player like the iPod. Though almost anyone can create a podcast, the most frequently downloaded podcasts come from news outlets, radio shows, famed commentators, and public figures.

Podcasting: use of "RSS" (see entry below) technology to create an audio file for the Internet that can be listened to on a computer or a digital music player.

Point-and-click: see "click."

Poke: more noncommittal than a message and more private than a wall post, a Facebook "poke" is a virtual wave "hello" from one user to another.

Portable document format: a document file type which opens with Adobe Acrobat Reader software and retains the document's original formatting. "PDF" is also used as a verb to describe the act of converting a

Word document into a PDF document (for example, "Please PDF the document before sending to the client.").

POS: an acronym for "parent over shoulder." "POS" is used by children to warn conversational partners to censor their dialogue because an authoritative figure is near. "POS" is usually a response to a "helicopter parent" (see entry above).

Profile: a standard used by social networking sites, a "profile" contains one's personal information including name, birthday, marital status, interests, hobbies, employment, and so on.

Reboot: to restart a computer, for example, "I will send you an e-mail after 'I reboot' my computer." The word can also be used in other verb forms such as "rebooting," "rebooted," etc.

Rebooted: see "reboot."

Rebooting: see "reboot."

Reply icon: a person can choose to respond to an e-mail he or she has received by clicking on the "reply" icon.

Retweet: used on Twitter, the term (abbreviated as "RT") indicates to followers that one is sharing content previously posted by another user. To "retweet" content, one's tweet should include "RT" @username with the username being the Twitter "handle" (entry above) of the person whose message one is "retweeting."

Retweeting: see "retweet."

Right click: see "click"

ROTFL: acronym for "rolling on the floor laughing"; it is used in text messages or instant messages to describe an intense state of laughter, and is a degree above the laughter described by "LOL" but about equal to that described by "LMAO" (see entries above).

RSS: see "RSS Feed."

RSS feed: meaning "Really Simple Syndication," a method of redistributing online content from multiple sources into a single outlet, either on a website or personal web browser. By subscribing to RSS feeds, users are able to access content without needing to visit a website, and are able to tailor and limit their daily media intake.

RT: see "retweet."

Screen: see "monitor."

Screen name: synonymous with a "user name" or a "handle" (see pertinent entries), a "screen name" is a person's identifier online, most frequently used in the context of instant messaging. For example, in the movie *You've Got Mail*, Tom Hanks' character, Joe Fox, uses NY152 as his screen name.

Screen saver: a series of images or revolving graphics that appears when a computer has been inactive for a period of time but is still on.

Search engine: hierarchical index of websites, which can be browsed by using keywords and search strings. Among the most frequently used search engines are Google, Yahoo!, and Bing.

SEO: see "Search Engine Optimization."

Search Engine Optimization: an online marketing strategy for businesses (or individuals) to increase website visibility and traffic. "SEO" includes adding relevant keywords as tags to web pages and creating hyperlinks to other highly visited websites.

Sext: a sexually suggestive or explicit message that is often accompanied by a picture or video. "Sexting," or the sending of such texts, became public knowledge when it was featured in the news as a disturbingly popular practice among teenagers. Due to the ease of digital reproduction, such messages are often distributed to people beyond the intended recipient much to the chagrin of the recipient.

Sexting: see "sext."

Share: By clicking on the icon "share," web users can distribute to other users almost all web content they come across on various websites, including personal, commercial, and social networking sites. In this context, "sharing" denotes the act of recommending content to others.

Sharing: see "share."

Short messaging service: pathway used to send text messages via a wireless device.

Smartphones: a type of cell phone that includes features similar to a "PDA" (see entry above) and a computer such as Internet access, an electronic appointment book, an electronic address book, and thousands of downloadable applications. Examples include the iPhone and BlackBerry.

SMS: acronym for "short messaging service."

SMSing: an expression used more frequently outside the United States to refer to the act of sending text messages, or "texting."

Social media: websites that build relationships and allow for interaction between users such as Twitter, Facebook, MySpace, LinkedIn, etc. These are also called "social networking sites."

Social networking: virtual networking that functions in the same way as networking in "real life." "Social networking" involves using the virtual space to cultivate a public persona, grow a network of personal and professional contacts, and forge new relationships.

Social networking sites: see "social media."

Software: similar to the brain of a human body, a computer's "software" maintains proper functioning of its "hardware" (system software), and directs the interaction between the computer and its user (application software).

Spam: the electronic equivalent of junk mail, e.g. unsolicited mass mailings.

Spyware: hidden software unknowingly downloaded to a computer that tracks and transmits web browsing habits to marketers, who then create a consumer profile for that computer and tailor marketing messages accordingly.

Status: see "status update."

Status update: a user-generated message published to the social networking site Facebook, that is posted to that user's profile and to the "news feed" of his or her "friends." A "status update" is to Facebook what a "tweet" is to Twitter.

Support: in the context of the web and cell phones, "support" has come to mean "technological support," system support, or customer support available online or via text messaging.

Surf: denotes spending time exploring different websites on the Internet. A popular phrase that developed early on, "surfing" or "surfing the net," or spending time online, alludes to the flow of information that a user encounters on the web.

Surfing: see "surf."

Surfing the net: see "surf."

Synched up: see "synchronization."

Synchronization: the process of transmitting information between a desktop or laptop and a mobile device so that they contain the same information; in "net lingo" (see entry above), this is also called being "synched up."

System software: see "software."

Text messaging: an electronic communication service available on cell phones and smartphones that transmits brief, typed messages between users; this is also called "texting" and, in some parts of the world, "SMSing" (see entry above).

Texting: see "text messaging."

TMI: acronym for "too much information"; it is used in conversation to acknowledge the disclosure of intimate details, and acts as a synonym for "inappropriate" (for example, "this may be TMI, but . . .").

Traffic: the number of people visiting a website is known as "traffic" or "web traffic"; it can be measured using web tracking software.

TTFN: acronym for "ta ta for now" used as a farewell in online and text conversation.

TTYL: more casual than "goodbye," it is a well-known acronym for "talk to you later."

Tweet: see "Twitter."

Tweeting: see "Twitter."

Twitter: a social networking website that can be accessed on a computer or a mobile device through which users publish brief, electronic messages (less than 160 characters) known as "tweets." Twitter users amass "followers," or people who subscribe to their "tweets." When you "follow" another Twitter user, their tweets show up on your Twitter homepage. Sending an update or communicating on Twitter is called "tweeting," for example, "though tempting, refrain from tweeting every few minutes to avoid annoying others."

Upload: opposite of "download," to "upload" something means to make it available online by sending it from a computer to a shared network such as the Internet. Sharing information on a social networking site such as a profile picture, photo album, or resume is made possible by "uploading " those computer files to the website.

URL: see "web address."

User friendly: describes a well-designed program or website that is easy for an amateur to navigate in computer terminology.

Username: one of two parts of the standard login information to access a secure website (the other is a "password"). Can also be called "screen name," "handle," or "e-mail address" (see entries above).

Vanity page: another name for a personal "homepage." Many artists and entrepreneurs maintain a vanity page to facilitate publicity, outreach, and sales.

Viral: a popular e-mail or video clip is known as having gone "viral" when it gets feverishly forwarded from one person to the next until it has reached millions. For instance in 2009, a video clip of a wedding party dancing down the church aisle to Chris Brown's song "Forever" went viral, and was even spoofed on an episode of the television show *The Office*.

Virtual: a simulation, that is almost real, but not in a tangible sense. The Internet is a "virtual" environment where people can engage in experiences without physically doing so (for example, cybersex). Virtual reality games like "The Sims" are popular because they allow users to adopt other identities and act in ways they might not in "real" life.

Virus: also called "computer virus," a malicious file or program that may enter a computer in a number of ways, notably through Internet activity such as downloading e-mail attachments from unknown senders, downloading online files, or installing programs with hidden "malware" (see entry above). Without virus protection software, a virus could destroy a computer's files, programs, or even the entire hard drive.

Wall post: a message from one individual to another published to the recipient's personal Facebook profile.

Web address: also known as a "URL," Uniform Resource Locator, the web address is the location of a web page on the Internet. For example, the web address of the Jobs Section of the *New York Times* is http://jobmarket.nytimes.com/pages/jobs

Webcasting: broadcasting for the web made possible by streaming media technology. Not only do traditional media outlets present webcasts, but ordinary people can as well using social media like *YouTube* whose slogan is "Broadcast Yourself."

Webinar: an interactive seminar accessed online, usually as a Powerpoint presentation accompanied by an instant messaging component and/or a telephone conference call.

Webisode: a play on the word "episode," it is a television episode made specifically for the Internet. Most American "webisodes" are made for television programming with a teenage audience, but they are also popular for adult programming in foreign markets.

Weblog: commonly known as a "blog," the "weblog" is an online diary or e-journal that anyone can create through a hosting service such as Blog-spot or Wordpress. The blogging phenomenon has transformed the pro-duction and delivery of the news by leveling the playing field, so to speak. At times, content produced by "amateur" bloggers is even given more credence than traditional news outlets for providing information unadul-terated by corporate interests.

Website: the Internet is comprised of millions of websites, each of which contains numerous web pages.

Webtraffic: see "traffic."

Widget: an application designed for use on a website. Live chat boxes, photo slide shows, interactive games, and online music players are exam-ples of this word.

Wi-Fi: wireless network that allows one to connect to the Internet without a cable or modem plugged into the computer.

Wired: to be connected and at ease with technology. Today's youth are known as the "wired generation" since many have daily contact with a television, an iPod, a cell phone, and the Internet.

ZIP disc: the modern "floppy disc," a "ZIP disc" is an external data storage device capable of storing and transporting up to two gigabytes of data, which is comparable to the storage capacity of a computer hard drive.

CONCEPTUAL AND TECHNICAL IMPLICATIONS

The foregoing glossary of terms, phrases, abbreviations, and colloquialisms emerging from and related to the pervasive use of cell phones and the Inter-net most likely falls short of being exhaustive. It is certainly possible that we have inadvertently omitted some deserving and well-known entries; others might have eluded the net we cast by the virtue of being region-specific (e.g., "texting" in USA is "SMSing" in India) and not prevalent in the United States, the terrain of our primary concern. Omissions of either variety, however, do not detract from our offering an over two-hundred word list that a new language has indeed emerged in relation to the cyberworld.

The questions that follow the establishment of this fact pertain to its significance. What are the intrapsychic and social reverberations of this new language? And, how do these impact upon the conduct of psychotherapy and psychoanalysis? As far as the first question is concerned, our answer is that the psychosocial impact of the cell phone Internet-related phraseology is powerful and manifold. The introduction of neologisms (e.g., "Googled," "sexting") creates a lexical layer in the psyche that remains relatively devoid of rich associations. These words exist (and will continue to exist for some time) on a denotative level. They lack connotative powers and their frequent use results in a peculiar pallor of language organization. On the other hand, by giving new meanings to old words (e.g. "chat," "friend"), the cell phone-Internet lexicon has enlarged the network of their associations. As a result, more and different ideas can emerge in the mind when such words are often spoken and heard. Further twist to these linguistic ups and downs is given by the acronyms (e.g. "GNOC" for "get naked on camera," "IMHO" for "in my honest opinion") and new ways of spelling words (e.g., UR for "you are," GR8 for "great") that is rampant in the cyber-culture. Working in unison, these four features of the cyber-language (neologisms, acronyms, additional meanings of old words, and new spellings) create a sector of the mind that stands apart from one regulated by the customary linguistic rules. The result is a newly born bilingualism.

The impact of this on the process and conduct of psychotherapy and psychoanalysis is evident in many ways. First and foremost, one becomes aware of the language discrepancy that exists when one partner in the clinical dyad is more proficient and/or more absorbed in the world of cell phones and the Internet. If the more "cyber-absorbed" partner is the patient, then some of his expressions might not be familiar to the analyst. Under such circums'tances, it is best to ask for an explanation though, of course, if the usage of unfamiliar words acquires a resistance or drive discharge quality (e.g., exhibitionism, sadism), the correct approach would be along the lines of interpretation. A second complication is caused by the new network of associations created by fresh words and novel ways of using old words. For instance, the word "seminar" has phonic relationships with "seminal," "seminole," and "semen" which the new word "webinar" (see description above) does not. The latter evokes memories of "webbed," "website," and "weeble." This difference has implications for the flow of free associations during the analytic hour. It can also impact upon the formation of dream images. An analysand who is serious about a "seminar," for instance, is likely to visually represent the event differently than one who is worried about a "webinar."

Similarly an analysand who is afraid of not having proper "etiquette" might dream of misspelling the word "etcetera" while the one who is worried about his "netiquette" might dream of casting a wide "net" on the sea.

The newly emergent acronyms (e.g. "LOL" for "laugh out loud" and "LMAO" for "laughing my ass off") and the innovative spellings used by the contemporary Internet, texting, and e-mail buffs (e.g., UR for "you are," LUV for "love") can also divert the chain of associations in unpredictable directions. This has to be kept in mind while listening to such patients in analysis and/or intensive psychotherapy.

Yet another variable in this realm is the impact of re-formulated narratives of "classics" from literature that populate cyberspace and videogames. Dante's *Inferno*, for instance, has been translated, transliterated, and unabashedly transformed for its video/web incarnation (Itzkoff, 2010). Its hero is no longer an introspective poet; he is a knight who, upon returning from the Crusades, finds his beloved Beatrice brutally murdered. What impact such recast versions of "classics" have on the mind which might simultaneously contain their original versions, remains to be seen. The potential of its causing a certain split and disharmony of representations and narratives is evident, though. And, what would happen if the analysand is familiar only with the current version and the analyst is devoted to the original? Such conundrums can complicate the therapeutic dialogue in subtle (and, at times, not so subtle) ways. They can also impact upon the analyst's countertransference feelings and attitudes. Kogan's (1999) acknowledgment of feeling intense envy of her young patient who was more proficient in Romanian, the original language shared by the analyst and the analysand before they migrated to Israel, comes to mind in this context. Could an older analyst who is less knowledgeable in computer-related matters be vulnerable to a similar countertransference pitfall while dealing with a computer savvy analysand of today's time? Could the distance between them vis-à-vis such language add to and/or stand for the ordinary and expectable generational and oedipal tensions between them? Although data to confirm or refute such speculations is currently unavailable, the situation is sure to change as time passes and more clinical material involving the Internet accrues. One would then be able to clearly assess the true technical significance of these preliminary hypotheses.

CONCLUDING REMARKS

In this contribution, we have focused upon the new language that has emerged as a concomitant, corollary, and consequence of the ubiquitous Internet and cell phone use in our current era. We have provided a comprehensive list of words, terms, phrases, abbreviations, acronyms, neologisms, and colloquialisms from this burgeoning lexicon. Our aim has been to (i) familiarize mental health professionals with a verbal register that has only recently gathered momentum and is certain to inch its way into the therapeutic discourse, (ii) prepare psychotherapists and psychoanalysts to anticipate and deal with technical challenges that can result from their patients using this new language, and (iii) lay down some groundwork for further investigation of this particular dimension of the cyber world. We hope that, in this way, we have made a contribution to the field of psycholinguistics.

Chapter Two

Minds on Media: Implications for Young People in the Internet Age

Joanne Cantor

This chapter examines the impact of the media in several areas. First, it presents recent data on young people's use of media, describing the major ways in which this use has expanded over the last decade and some recently reported correlations between media use and negative outcomes. Then, to illuminate some of the processes underlying media effects, it presents a summary of the literature on the impact of media violence on both aggression and fear. In addition, based on the observation that new media have exploded the incidence of multitasking among youth, some new research on the impact of multitasking is presented. In all areas, findings in neurophysiology impart a deeper understanding of the observed effects. The chapter ends by outlining some principles for generating practical guidance for caregivers and mental health providers.

Concern over children's exposure to electronic media goes at least as far back as the 1930s when researchers worried about the impact of radio and movies on children (Blumer, 1933; Dysinger and Ruckmick, 1933; Eisenberg, 1936). The role of the media in young people's lives has changed continuously as new forms of media, particularly television, have been popularized, and research on television and children has burgeoned since the 1950s (Wartella and Robb, 2008). The emergence of computers and the Internet and the recent wholesale adoption of portable electronic devices by young people have added new dimensions to the role of the media in young people's lives.

THE CHANGED LANDSCAPE OF TECHNOLOGY FOR YOUTH

It seems difficult to overestimate the role of media technology in the lives of youth today. A recent national survey by the Kaiser Family Foundation was characterized by the following headline in the *New York Times*: "If Your Kids Are Awake, They're Probably Online" (Lewin, 2010). According to the Kaiser report (Rideout, Foehr, and Roberts, 2010), media consumption by eight to eighteen-year-olds has surged dramatically over the past five years. Not including school-related uses, the average young person spends seven hours and thirty-eight minutes per day consuming media. This figure has increased 27 percent since 2004. Because 29 percent of their media use involves multitasking, young people are actually consuming, on average, ten hours and forty-five minutes of media content per day (up from 8:33 in 2004). Exposure to music, television, computers, and video games has increased significantly, while exposure to print media has not increased. Young people have easy access to these technologies outside of their parents' control: 20 percent of media consumption occurs on mobile devices; 71 percent of youth have a television in their bedroom; 76 percent own an iPod or MP3 player; 66 percent have a cell phone; and 59 percent have a portable video game player.

This astonishing expansion of media exposure, especially exposure that is not likely to be controlled or observed by adults, makes it all the more important to understand its impact on children's health and well-being. In spite of a wealth of research on media effects, however, much of the public does not understand what it means.

WHY MEDIA EFFECTS ARE HARD TO COMMUNICATE

One reason research on the impact of the media on youth is misunderstood by the general public has to do with research methodology. Although the public often expects to hear about clear-cut cause-and-effect relationships, the processes by which media affect consumers are often long-term and complex. It is not possible to randomly assign children early in their lives to consume different amounts and types of media and then years later see how these children turned out. But the same type of limitation also exists for medical research that we often accept more readily. It is not feasible to randomly assign groups of people to smoke differing amounts of cigarettes for years, and then count the number of people who developed cancer.

Medical researchers studying the effects of tobacco conduct correlational studies in which they look at the amount people have smoked during their lives and then chart the rate at which they have succumbed to cancer. They control statistically for other factors, of course—other healthy and unhealthy behaviors that either reduce or promote the tendency to develop cancer. Then they can find out whether smoking contributed to cancer, over and above these other influences. And since they cannot do experiments injecting people with carcinogens to determine if they cause cancer, they use animal studies. These studies are artificial, but they tell us something about the short-term effects of tobacco that cannot be found from correlational studies. Putting the correlational studies and experiments together, we now have powerful data about the effects of smoking on the development of cancer.

Similarly, media researchers do longitudinal studies of children's media exposure and look at the types of behaviors they engage in over time. They also control for other factors, such as early influences, family problems, and the like. They do not look at media exposure in a vacuum; they examine whether there is a correlation between media and later outcomes, even controlling for other influences. They also do experiments. Like the animal experiments for cancer, these often create unnatural situations, but such experiments fill the gaps that cannot be filled otherwise. Experiments are often designed to show short-term effects that we know increase the likelihood of later outcomes.

A second reason for the misunderstanding of media-effects research is that media industries are immensely profitable and they spend enormous amounts of time and money arguing that their products are not harmful. In addition, they control the mainstream media, the most powerful means of promoting their arguments. Therefore, when media lobbyists or apologists call into question scientifically reliable findings from independent researchers, this creates enough confusion on the part of parents to blunt the impact of worrisome findings. Moreover, since young people love their media and do not want to be restricted, the apparent confusion makes it even harder for parents and caregivers to adopt and enforce sensible rules and policies that might promote healthy media use.

MEDIA USE PER SE

Independent of the content they choose to consume, does the sheer time spent consuming media have implications? Although the data are correlational, the Kaiser Family Foundation study reported that heavy media use was associated with lower grades. For example, survey respondents were divided into three groups based on their use of media. Heavy users (21 percent of the sample) consumed more than sixteen hours a day of media content; moderate users (63 percent) consumed between three and sixteen hours per day; and light users (17 percent) consumed less than three hours. Reports of receiving low grades were highest among heavy media users: 44 percent of heavy users, 31 percent of moderate users, and 23 percent of light users said they received fair or poor grades. The only type of media exposure that was higher among youth with good grades was reading for pleasure.

Amount of media use was also related to measures of personal contentment in the Kaiser Study. Combining items assessing having many friends, getting along with parents, being happy at school, and rarely getting into trouble or being bored or sad, respondents who were the least content spent more time with media (thirteen hours and six minutes, on average) than those who were the most content (eight hours and forty-four minutes). The analyses relating both academic success and contentment to media use controlled for other factors, such as age, gender, race, parent education, and single vs. two-parent households. Still, these data do not necessarily implicate a causal connection between media consumption and negative outcomes. It is possible that unhappy and unsuccessful young people turn to media for substitute gratification. In fact, it is likely that these relationships are circular. However, the content that young people consume is undoubtedly a factor in any effects.

MEDIA VIOLENCE AS AN EXAMPLE

The media present a vast array of content types that influence young people in a variety of ways. One of the areas that has been studied the most is that of media violence. Although other areas can be argued to be equally important, many of the processes involved in media violence effects work similarly for other content areas. Therefore, using media violence as an example can illuminate other effects as well.

One reason that the media violence issue is especially fraught with controversy is that most public discussions of the problem focus on criminal violence and ignore other unhealthy outcomes that affect many more children. In other words, although a small portion of children may actually become criminally violent as a function of media exposure, many more children may increase their feelings of hostility, become desensitized to the harms that violence causes, or become unnecessarily fearful. These less publicly visible outcomes may lead some children to become violent. But even those who do not become violent are harmed by these consequences. Similarly, it would be wrong to limit the study of the outcomes of exposure to sex on TV to whether or not it promotes teen pregnancy. Even if a teenager does not become pregnant (or impregnate someone), televised depictions of sex may alter young people's anxiety levels regarding sex, their concerns about sexually transmitted disease, their attitudes toward monogamy, or their views of healthy relationships, and so forth.

Effects of Media Violence on Aggression

In understanding the effects of media violence on aggression, the question is not whether media violence *causes* violence, but whether viewing violence contributes to the likelihood that someone will commit violence or increases the severity of violence when it is committed. The most direct and obvious way in which viewing violence contributes to violent behavior is through imitation or social learning. There is a wealth of psychological research demonstrating that learning often occurs through imitation, and most parents know that children imitate televised words and actions from an early age. Media apologists, who cannot deny that imitation sometimes happens, try to argue that the effects are trivial because children know better than to imitate anything that is really harmful. We are all familiar with incidents in which criminal and lethal violence has had an uncanny resemblance to a scene in a movie. However, any crime is the result of many influences acting together, and skeptics and even researchers will point out that isolated anecdotes cannot be generalized to society at large. Because most children are so fully immersed in our media culture, it is usually difficult to link a specific media program to a specific harmful outcome, even though some similarities between media scenarios and subsequent acts seem too close to be considered coincidences.

Once in a while researchers get the chance to conduct a "natural experiment" that makes a vivid and compelling point in a systematic and rigorous fashion. This happened in the mid 1990s in Israel, shortly after *World Wrestling Federation* (now called *World Wrestling Entertainment*) was introduced to Israeli TV. Noting news reports that this program had resulted in a crisis of playground injuries in schools, a researcher at Tel Aviv University conducted a nationwide survey of elementary school principals, with follow-up questionnaires of teachers and students in selected schools (Lemish, 1997). What Lemish found was that more than half of the principals responding to her survey reported that WWF-type fighting had created problems in their schools. The principals had no trouble distinguishing the imitative behavior they were suddenly seeing from the martial-arts type behaviors that had occurred prior to the arrival of WWF. The new behaviors occurred during recess-time re-creations of specific wrestling matches that had aired, and included banging heads, throwing opponents to the floor and jumping onto them from furniture, poking their eyes with fingers, pulling their hair, and grabbing their genital areas. Almost half of the responding principals reported that these new behaviors had necessitated first aid within the school, and almost one-fourth reported injuries (including broken bones, loss of consciousness, and concussions) that required emergency room visits or professional medical care. Although most of the children involved were old enough to know that the wrestling they were watching was fake, this knowledge did not stop many of them from trying out the moves themselves. The mayhem continued throughout Israel until programmers agreed to reduce the frequency with which WWF appeared, and until schools initiated media literacy programs designed to counteract the program's effects.

Desensitization

Simply copying what is seen in the media is only one means by which viewing violence contributes to unhealthy outcomes among youth. Another commonly discussed psychological process is desensitization. Desensitization occurs when an emotional response is repeatedly evoked in situations in which the action tendency that is associated with the emotion proves irrelevant or unnecessary. For example, most people become emotionally aroused when they see a snake slithering toward them. The physiological response they are experiencing is part of what is called the "flight or fight" reaction—an innate tendency that prepares an organism to do what it needs to do when it is threatened. But the individual who spends a good deal of time around harmless, nonpoisonous snakes knows there is no need to retreat or attack the animal, and over time the body "learns" not to experience increased heart rate, blood pressure, or other physiological concomitants of fear at the sight of snakes. In a somewhat analogous fashion, exposure to media violence, particularly that which entails bitter hostilities or the graphic display of injuries, initially induces an intense emotional reaction in viewers. Over time and with repeated exposure in the context of entertainment and relaxation, however, many viewers exhibit decreasing emotional responses to the depiction of violence and injury. Studies have documented that desensitization results in reduced arousal and emotional disturbance while witnessing violence (Cline, Croft, and Courrier, 1973). More disturbingly, studies have reported that desensitization leads children to wait longer to call an adult to intervene in a witnessed physical fight between peers (Molitor and Hirsch, 1994) and results in a reduction of sympathy for the victims of domestic abuse (Mullin and Linz, 1995). Few people would argue that these are healthy outcomes. Today's youth have greater opportunities for desensitization to media violence than ever before. We now have so many television channels, so many movies on video, and so many video-, computer-, and Internet-based games available, that media-violence aficionados have a virtually limitless supply and can witness or manipulate intensely gruesome images repeatedly, often in the privacy of their own bedrooms.

Increases in Hostility

A third common outcome of viewing violence is an increase in hostile feelings. Some people argue that the well-substantiated correlation between chronic hostility and violence viewing simply shows that people who are already hostile are more likely to choose violence as entertainment. It is true that violent, hostile people are more attracted to media violence (Goldstein, 1998), but research shows that the relationship goes both ways. Researchers in Quebec went to a theater and asked moviegoers to fill out the Buss-Durkee hostility inventory either before or after they viewed a film that they themselves had selected (Black and Bevan, 1992). The findings showed that both the male and female viewers who had chosen the Chuck Norris action movie *Missing in Action*, were initially more hostile than the viewers who had selected the nonviolent drama *A Passage to India*, demonstrating that people who were more hostile to begin with were more likely to be attracted to a violent than a nonviolent film. Furthermore, viewers' levels of hostility increased after viewing the violent movie, but remained at a low level after viewing the nonviolent movie. This study once again disproves the sometimes popular notion of "catharsis," that violence viewing helps purge people of their hostile inclinations. To the contrary.

What are the consequences of this increased hostility after viewing violence? Often, it interferes with the ability to interact in interpersonal settings. One aspect of this effect has been termed an increased *hostile attribution bias*. In an experiment, nine- to eleven-year-old girls and boys were asked to play one of two video games (Kirsh, 1998). One was a nonviolent sports game called *NBA JAM:TE*; the other was a somewhat sanitized version of *MORTAL KOMBAT II*, a highly violent martial arts game. After playing the game, the children heard five stories involving provoking incidents in which the intention of the provoker was ambiguous. For example, in one story, a child was hit in the back with a ball, but it was unclear whether the person who threw the ball had done so on purpose or by accident. In answering questions after hearing the stories, the children who had just played the violent video game were more likely than those who had played the nonviolent game to attribute bad motives and negative feelings to the perpetrator, and to anticipate that they themselves would retaliate if they were in that situation. Participating in violence in fantasy apparently cast a negative cloud over the children's views of interpersonal interactions

This increase in hostility is not necessarily short-lived. An experiment looked at the interpersonal consequences of repeated exposure to gratuitous violence in movies (Zillmann and Weaver, 1999). Researchers randomly assigned both male and female college students to view either nonviolent or intensely violent feature films four days in a row. On the fifth day, in a purportedly unrelated study, the participants were put in a position to help or hinder another person's chances of future employment. The surprising results indicated that both the men and the women who had received the recent daily dose of movie violence were more willing to undermine that person's job prospects, whether she had treated them well or had behaved in an insulting fashion. The repeated violence viewing apparently provided what the researchers termed *an enduring hostile mental framework* that damaged interactions that were affectively neutral as well as those that involved provocation.

These are just a few studies that illustrate some of the unhealthy effects of media violence. But how representative are these studies? Although media spokespersons argue that the findings are inconsistent, meta-analyses, which statistically combine the findings of all the studies on a particular topic, show otherwise. Meta-analyses of media violence in general, as well as those of violent video games, show a consistent association between exposure to media violence and a variety of antisocial behaviors (Anderson, 2004; Anderson and Bushman, 2001; Bushman and Anderson, 2001; Paik and Comstock, 1994). Further analyses have shown that the strength of the association between media violence and antisocial behavior is larger, for example, than the relationship between exposure to lead and low IQ in children, and almost twice as large as the relationship between calcium intake and bone density (Bushman and Anderson, 2001).

The Role of Mirror Neurons

Why is imitation of aggression so prevalent in young people? And why do they adopt feelings of hostility and hostile perceptions when watching media violence, even when they know what they are watching is only entertainment? We have known for a long time that children, and adults, too, often imitate what they see. But imitation has been a puzzle to psychologists. On one hand, when babies are born, their behavior is just a bundle of reflexes and random actions. They do not have much control over their muscles or behavior. But on the other hand, infants imitate very early. By the end of two weeks, they can match the facial expressions of their caretakers, sticking out their tongue when someone sticks their tongue out at them, for example (Meltzoff and Moore, 1977). Matching someone else's actions is a very complicated process. How do infants know which muscles in their own bodies will produce the same effect that they are seeing, and how do they engage those muscles?

An explanation comes from neurophysiology. In the past few decades, brain researchers have discovered *mirror neurons*—neurons that fire both when we perform an action and when we watch someone else perform that action (Iacoboni, 2008). These mirror neurons are located in an area of the brain known as the *premotor cortex*. This is the area of the brain that is involved in preparing for action. In some sense, when we watch other people in action, our brains "warming up" to copy that action. Mirror neurons respond involuntarily and automatically, and they respond to the emotional expressions of other people as well as to their overt physical movements. In essence, when we see someone else do something, or see them express an emotion, our brains mirror some of the activity of the brain of the person we are watching.

Mirror neurons may well account for the ability of infants to copy facial expressions. They also seem to underlie the process of empathy, the fact that we readily take on the emotions of other people. For example, research shows that when we watch someone else being poked with a needle, some of the same neurons fire that become active when a doctor pokes us with a needle (Ramachandran, 2006). Although there is still much to be discovered, the activity of mirror neurons suggests that our brains "pre-practice" any activity that we watch—perhaps making us ready to perform it ourselves. Another reason that mirror neurons are important can be derived from a popular expression in neuroscience: "neurons that fire together, wire together" (Shatz, 2006). This means that if a particular neural pathway is repeatedly fired in the brain, that pathway becomes stronger and stronger and more likely to fire in the future. So the effects of practice are not fleeting. We can establish and strengthen enduring neural pathways simply by watching other people.

Keep in mind that mirror neurons fire in response to all behaviors people watch. If they watch people performing healthy, prosocial behaviors, their mirror neurons will practice those behaviors. But if they spend hours and hours witnessing violence and hostility, it is those mirror neurons that will receive the practice and those neural pathways that will be strengthened. In other words, our brains absorb what we watch and there are physical traces in the brain that result. The bottom line is: if a young person (or anyone, in fact) watches much media violence, their aggression and hostility mirror neurons will be well exercised.

Fears, Anxieties, and Sleep Disturbances

Although most of researchers' attention has focused on how media violence affects the aggression-related behaviors of children and adolescents, there is growing evidence that violence viewing also induces intense fears and anxieties in young viewers. For example, a survey of more than 2,000 third through eighth graders in Ohio revealed that as the number of hours of television viewing per day increased, so did the prevalence of symptoms of psychological trauma, such as anxiety, depression, and posttraumatic stress (Singer et al., 1998). Similarly, a survey of the parents of almost 500 children in kindergarten through fourth grade in Rhode Island revealed that the amount of children's television viewing (especially television viewing at bedtime) and having a television in one's own bedroom were significantly related to the frequency of sleep disturbances (Owens et al., 1999). Indeed, 9 percent of the parents surveyed reported that their child experienced TV-induced nightmares at least once a week. Finally, a random national survey reported that 62 percent of parents with children between the ages of two and seventeen said that their child had been frightened by something they had seen in a TV program or movie (Gentile and Walsh, 1999).

For the most part, what frightens children in the media involves violence or the perceived threat of violence or harm. It is important to note, however, that parents often find it difficult to predict children's fright reactions to television and films because a child's level of cognitive development influences how he or she perceives and responds to media stimuli (Cantor, 1998, 2009). For example, young children are likely to be frightened by make-believe characters with grotesque features, whether they are violent or not. As children mature cognitively, they become less disturbed by fantasy and more prone to be frightened by real-world threats, although supernatural themes still haunt many teenagers and even adults.

What is especially intriguing about the frightening effects of media is how long lasting they sometimes are. Two independently conducted studies of college students' retrospective reports of having been frightened by a television show or movie demonstrate that the presence of vivid, detailed memories of enduring media-induced fear is nearly universal (Harrison and Cantor, 1999; Hoekstra, Harris, and Helmick, 1999). Many research participants report phobia-like reactions, such as disturbances in eating or sleeping, mental preoccupation with the disturbing material, and subsequent avoidance or dread of the depicted situation. In one of these studies, more than one-fourth of the respondents said that the impact of the program or movie (viewed an average of six years earlier) was still with them at the time of reporting (Harrison and Cantor, 1999).

When adults are asked to describe an incidence of media-induced fear, many describe the program or movie and their intense reactions in vivid detail, even though the event had occurred many years earlier. What is intriguing is how frequently people describe what appear to be irrational long-term reactions. For example, the following are typical of enduring responses to some well-known movies:

> "Needless to say I didn't venture very far out into the ocean. Even the swimming pool at the campground made me a bit apprehensive ... For a long time I would associate any body of water with sharks." —*Jaws*

> "I now hate watching the shadow of the trees outside of my bedroom window. Even now, I certainly don't leave my TV on after the station goes off the air, and I still always make sure that my closet door is closed before I go to sleep." —*Poltergeist*

"For almost two years this had such an impact on me that I would never take a shower unless the curtain was three-fourths open so I could see in the mirror across from the shower that no one else was in the bathroom. I even locked the door at all times. But even that wasn't enough, so I also pulled out the drawer alongside the door so in case someone got the door unlocked, they wouldn't be able to open the door past the drawer." —*Psycho*

It is not surprising that a young child would be frightened by images of bloody violence or monstrous-looking creatures, but what seems perplexing is that so many adults still experience fear years after exposure. Why does an adult still worry about sharks in pools, televisions, trees, fictional characters? These adults should know full well that they are not in danger. Why do these feelings persist?

Research on the neurophysiology of fear can illuminate these reactions. To oversimplify greatly, two separate brain regions are important in the fear response: the forebrain (or prefrontal cortex), which is responsible our conscious thoughts and reasoning, and the amygdala, a small almond-shaped area that is very important for emotions. According to Joseph LeDoux (1996), the foremost researcher on the neurobiology of fear, when you have an intense fright reaction, both the forebrain and the amygdala are involved. The amygdala responds first and creates the fight-or-flight reaction to fear: your muscles tense, your heart rate and respiration increase, and various hormones like adrenaline are released into your bloodstream. Your forebrain takes more time to react in consciously evaluating whatever it was that frightened you. According to LeDoux, because fear is an emotion strongly linked to survival, there are two important aspects of the way our brain works in fear. First, it reacts fast—if something threatens your life, you cannot be slow to react. And second, if you survive that life-threatening event, your brain wants to make sure that you vividly remember what threatened you, because you may not be so lucky the next time. Therefore, according to LeDoux, traumatic fear memories need to be strong and long-lasting.

Research shows that although our conscious memories of traumatizing situations are not always correct and are quite malleable over time, implicit fear memories that are stored in the amygdala are highly resistant to change. In fact, LeDoux says that they are "indelible." Applying this reasoning to the media situation, when you are reminded of a movie like *Jaws* that frightened you as a child, your forebrain should bring up the interpretations you have had in the intervening years—how silly you were to be so frightened by that obviously mechanical shark, and so on. But your amygdala will send out those fight-or-flight signals that get your body agitated again. Even though you may be swimming in a pool and your forebrain may be reiterating the fact that there are no sharks in pools and there is no danger, your amygdala ensures that you are anxious, tense, and uncomfortable in the water. LeDoux maintains that when your forebrain and your amygdala disagree with one another in this situation, the amygdala usually wins. You have to keep repeating your conscious thoughts to calm yourself down, but your amygdala can be very persistent in stirring up the bodily reactions that make you feel stressed even though in your mind, you are safe.

Here are some typical examples of people describing their bodies reacting to memories of movies, even though they know they are not in danger:

"I am actually getting flushed even writing this paper because I am so worked up as I picture the images that I remember in my head." —*ET*

"My spine continues to crawl today at the thought of *The Wizard of Oz*."

The interesting thing about these responses is that although people know that what they saw was just a movie, their amygdala seems to react as though it had been a real, traumatic experience.

THE IMPACT OF MULTITASKING

As technology has become more mobile, not only has the time spent using media increased, the amount of time multitasking has burgeoned. As indicated earlier, young people in the Kaiser study reported multitasking 29 percent of the time they used media. In addition, 27 percent of youth in that study reported multitasking "most of the time" while reading, and 31 percent reported multitasking most of the time while doing homework. Although the Kaiser report did not test the relationship between multitasking and contentment or academic performance, there is mounting evidence that multitasking is counterproductive.

Experts in information-processing and brain researchers have concluded that our brains cannot focus attention on two things at once. For example, molecular biologist John Medina (2008) says "it is literally impossible for our brains to multitask when it comes to paying attention." What is really happening when we seem to be multitasking is that we are rapidly switching our attention back and forth between tasks. Our brains are easily distracted by new input, and the controlled attention needed for reading, writing, and other school-related activities is especially difficult in a noisy environment that is full of distractions (Cantor, 2009).

Some people argue that young people can multitask more effectively than older adults, and there is some truth to this notion. The underlying factor is that they have a larger working memory capacity so they do not lose as much information every time they switch back and forth between two tasks (Klingborg, 2009). Some people have also argued that members of the current

, younger generation are better multitaskers because they have grown up in a cyberspace environment and their brains have been transformed by their digital experiences. However, new research suggests that this may be a false conclusion. One study (Ophir, Nass, and Wagner, 2009) tried to demonstrate that frequent multitaskers would perform better than infrequent multitaskers in situations involving two simultaneous tasks. However, to the surprise of the researchers, they found the opposite: frequent multitaskers performed more poorly on all three multitasking tests that were administered.

Another study (Foerde, Knowlton, and Poldrack, 2006) demonstrated that multitasking and single-tasking involve different brain processes and that learning while multitasking produces a lower level of understanding. Participants engaged in learning some things while single-tasking and other things while dual-tasking. When they were tested in a different context, performance was much worse for dual- than for single-tasked trials. Moreover, after multitasking, learners were much less able to identify the rules underlying what they were doing. Brain imaging revealed that different areas of the brain had been active under single-tasked as opposed to multitasked learning. Learning while multitasking involved implicit processes similar to forming a habit without consciousness of what was being learned. Learning while single-tasking involved utilizing working memory, and what was learned was more flexible and involved more abstract, generalizable knowledge.

In general, multitasking interferes with the accuracy and quality of the work being attempted. In a field study conducted in a natural learning environment (Fried, 2008), college students who used their laptops in class for multitasking had poorer overall class performance than those who did not. If young people insist that they are good at multitasking, they are probably wrong. They are voluntarily handicapping themselves.

IMPLICATIONS AND ADVICE FOR CAREGIVERS AND MENTAL HEALTH PROVIDERS

This chapter has focused on several negative effects of involvement in media on young people's well-being. But it would be incorrect to assume that all of the effects of media are negative. For example, there are many uplifting and educational television programs, movies, and video games. Moreover, some recent research suggests that adolescents' use of the Internet for communication with friends via instant messaging and other technologies enhances their feelings of connectedness and social well-being (Valkenburg and Peter, 2009). The effect of any technology clearly depends on how it is used, and a wide array of options currently exists for young people.

Because of the potential for harmful effects, it is certainly advisable for adults to be aware of and guide the media use of the young people in their care. Monitoring is growing more difficult all the time as communication devices are becoming more accessible. Keeping media out of children's bedrooms and placing computers in public spaces in the home are good policies. However, as devices become cheaper, smaller, and more mobile, these approaches become harder and harder to implement, particularly as children reach their teens.

For young children, however, keeping the bedroom free of media and restricting their access to inappropriately violent, scary, or sexual media contents is recommended. Parents should be advised to find out about television programs, movies, and video games in advance by looking at ratings, reviews, and online descriptions. Several websites (for example, screenit.com, commonsensemedia.org, kids-in-mind.com) provide useful information.

As children near their teen years, however, restricting access becomes complicated. This is because of what has come to be termed the "forbidden fruit" effect. When adolescents feel their freedom to choose media content is threatened, they often want to view it all the more (Bushman and Cantor, 2003; Nathanson, 2002). When guiding adolescents' exposure, it may be more effective to deliberate with them about their media choices before they view or to view with them and have discussions about the content (Chakroff and Nathanson, 2008). Helping young people understand the effects the media are having on them may be the best way to enlist their cooperation.

In the end, it is important to recognize that as the media play an increasingly important role in the lives of young people, and as new technologies and contents are being developed and promoted every day, the importance of understanding the impact of media on young people's health and welfare will only increase.

Chapter Three

The Epidemic of Information: Pros and Cons

John L. Frank

Dr. Joanne Cantor offers a very important piece of work and helps us think about the profound effects of media technology on today's youth. She discusses numerous studies showing that exposure to media violence and prolonged use of email, the internet, and smartphones, as well as multi-tasking, are taking a significant toll on the quality of our children's lives. Heavy media usage is correlated with aggressive and sometimes violent behavior, distractibility, fear, other dysphoric states, and decreased ability to empathize with others. While recognizing the benefits of digital technology, many join Dr. Cantor's concern that our culture's focus on efficiency and productivity are at the expense of the psychological growth of children.

The phrase "social media" is a little jarring to me. I haven't integrated the social worlds of people relating to each other in real space with media-driven social phenomena. I am of the generation that remembers that before television, there was a hand held mechanical media device consisting of seven small Kodachrome slides on a single circular cardboard that fit into a View Master. With each push of a lever, a new slide transported me to Mexico City, the Nile River, and the St. Louis Zoo for three dimensional viewing and my own reveries. When the microchip was being developed in the 70s, I was already a psychoanalytic candidate.

David Skorton (2010), president of Cornell University, responding to a recent series of suicides at Ivy League colleges, questioned how in a time of unrelenting connectivity, through Facebook, Twitter, and smartphones, we have lost our ability to "help our young people." Dr. Skorton suggests that these students were technologically savvy and electronically connected but their human connections failed. His letter, written two weeks ago, helps frame my remarks to Dr. Cantor's paper and today's conference.

In work with individual children and adolescents, I see two areas of overlap between Dr. Cantor's concerns about media technology and psychoanalytic developmental theory: the first, issues of *boundaries* and the second, *play and imagination.* I will comment about both.

First, the world of cyberspace has altered many traditional boundaries— work and play, serious discourse and entertainment, adulthood and childhood, and public and private. Parents and educators are concerned about teens sending nude pictures to each other (sexting), cyber-bullying, and troublesome flash mobs generated by cell phones. Is individual expression and originality compromised by a technology that encourages "borrowing" and enables plagiarism with simple digital clicks? The child's exposure to what traditionally had been adult prerogative has increased by handheld devices that are hidden from parents' view. Dr. Cantor points to how the young child's early unlimited access to "adult" news, views, and entertainment overwhelm brain and mind. The American Academy of Pediatrics mandates that infants have no screen experience before the age of two.

Over half a century ago, John Bowlby (1952) said it was "essential for the young child to experience a warm, intimate and continuous relationship with his mother where contradictory demands for unlimited love and revenge on her for not meeting his demands will become under the control of his developing personality." Bowlby's interest was to help governments, social workers, and psychiatrists see that maternal neglect leading to child behavior problems was as serious a public health issue as diphtheria and typhoid. Bowlby's message was as relevant at mid-century as it is in 2010.

In our rush for two-year-olds to become sixteen-year-olds, elementary schools are increasingly wired, and the Muppets Elmo and Cookie Monster have become part of the child's interactive world. Five-year-olds are asking for cell phones. Market researchers—under the guise of educating children to be competitive online—are trumping parent-child centered social interaction. Media emphasis on fashion for girls and power and destruction for boys encourages earlier separation from parents. For preteens and adolescents, identifying with "in" or "cool" peers is a way of seeking self-esteem outside of the family. Parents don't appreciate that behind challenges to their values and authority are often unacknowledged dependency longings and anxiety over these very separation conflicts.

Many parents may defer to their children's claims for unlimited access to social networks. Parents may be stymied, confused, and paralyzed. Some welcome their children's turn to social networks because it frees them to attend to their own pressing needs. It is not inevitable that media technologies diminish family bonds. Preoccupation with work and/or leisure activity is not new. At issue is how family members can be genuinely interested and concerned with each other, at levels of immediacy and intimacy that promote true mutuality. At the same time, parents have needs and interests that are not necessarily compatible with their children's. Adult activity that has content, time, and place is also important for children to witness, come up against, and respect including the boundary meaning of "off-limits." Without this, there is a risk that child-centered omnipotence will persist well into and beyond adolescence.

PLAY AND IMAGINATION

The act of imagining (what is not immediately available to the senses) is to psychoanalytic theory what electronic imagery is to cyberspace. The image of imagination is subjective, unique, and originates with the imaginer who decides if, when, and with whom to communicate. Imaginative space is perhaps a later form of what Donald Winnicott (1953) described as transitional space that balances real human connectedness with acts of separateness and loss. Transitional space contains feelings of early omnipotence transformed into cultural and communal acts (art, music, dance, literature, religion). How imaginative/transitional space and cyberspace differ may be important in appreciating the impact of social media on child development.

In Winnicott's "holding environment," creative imagination is what allows the small child to create something part real and part imaginary-fantasy. In face-to-face interaction (Brazelton, 1992; Tronick, 2001), intimacy is spawned. Mother provides doses of objective reality (her breast, milk, hair, gaze, voice, warmth, blankets, toys) which the child takes or leaves, building memories of mutual regulation as psychic structure. Transitional space is safe for the infant to experience highly intense emotions such as anxiety, dependence, helplessness, hatred, and revenge, but also curiosity, excitement, and joy. It is also the first place and time where the infant—under maternal supervision—can successfully feel alone with its feelings without undue anxiety. The roots of this early developmental achievement—the capacity to be alone—may well be an important resiliency factor in allowing older children to manage being by themselves sometimes without being plugged into multiple sources of ongoing stimulation. For parents to provide the minimal environmental provisions to their children, the caregivers also need to be able to tolerate negative affect states (anxiety, hatred, disappointment), be able to view the world from a multicentric position. Fantasy and creative play are dependent on secure early relationships and are the building blocks of trust, competence, and self-esteem. Relational rhythms learned in a secure attachment are sought after with other family members and then peers as the child engages with reliable others beyond mother. The unavailable parent may force the child into premature adulthood or into a desperate effort to avoid growing up through a Peter Pan-like existence.

Freud (1920) was one of the first to point out that children's play was a natural self-healing activity. It allows children to turn passive experiences into active ones where they can try out changing the end of the story. This is a far cry from the unimaginative choices that media directors give children to "customize" their online experiences! Imaginative play by children in small groups allows the transmission of jokes, stories, and both culture and counter-culture messages. Creative play fosters small and large muscle activity, perceptual-motor skills, cooperation, rivalry, leadership, and the working through of peer problems. Small children, in their own play and with others, represent feelings, wishes, motives, defenses, and pretenses that free the child from the concrete sensory-perceptual world of "what you see is what you get." As captain, acrobat, lion tamer, inventor, engineer, and entertainer, trial-and-error performances without requiring an "end product" are emotionally satisfying and further self-reliance.

While learning, practicing, and excelling are admirable values for young people, their combination with digital connectedness in child and parent contrasts markedly with "down time"—where children are with family or friends in a "relaxed" frame of mind. A generation ago, children went out to play after school. But to many adults now, "free" play is seen as an irrelevant recreation rather than an important multi-purpose activity for children to learn and adapt to the real world. Down time is when people hang out, refuel their inner life, pretend, have fun, and daydream; "tell me your wishes and I'll tell you mine," storytelling where imagination ties fact and fiction together; tales that are funny, surprising, sad, upsetting, exhilarating, poignant, or humbling. Familiarity grew out of spontaneous contacts in neighborhoods and on porches. Grandparents, neighbors, and other family members visited and talked. There were picnics and communal celebrations and also coming together to grieve. For thirty years until 2001, earnest Mr. Rogers in his popular TV show took a full minute to change into his sneakers and sweater while speaking warmly and directly to children about their feelings and how each of them was special.

I see risks to development from our digital culture. I see more difficulty for children and families to relate to one another with intimacy and familiarity coming from a serious interest in personal and family narrative, and a sharing of and working through of a range of human emotions. Familiarity and intimacy require personal face-to-face exchange in real time! It is true that for some—frightened of the intensity and responsibility of real relationships—the distance built into online relationships may protect against the anxiety of closeness. One very shy, awkward adolescent girl told me how pleased she was to have found a small group of "friends" each of whom created a character type they could inhabit online allowing interchanges that seemed impossible in real life. But for others—and I am thinking here again of Dr. Skorton's letter, I suspect the excitement of manipulating sources of sensory stimulation, the quick pleasures of cyberspace entertainment, and virtual "friendships" do not replace reliable people where serious and heart-felt sentiments can be shared. An added pain might be the lack of conscious awareness of their longings for relatedness which is central to many adoles-cents' depression. Some may have been retreating from real to virtual rela-tionships for most of their lives.

A few thoughts about treatment. In line with Dr. Cantor's assessment, I think we should advocate for preventive intervention including and especial-ly the value of face-to-face family time where media devices are unplugged! When I was first learning about psychotherapy with children, a supervisor said to me: "Avoid those Monopoly board games with all the pieces like the plague. You'll get so caught up in the structure of the game you'll loose focus on what really matters!" I suppose electronic media carry the same risk in the consultation room. But I've had kids read books or silently draw geometrical forms to avoid talking and I've only had one preadolescent girl sit with her back to me while spending the session texting her friends.

CLINICAL EXAMPLES

I want to end with three brief clinical vignettes in which media technology is present but did not become a barrier to the therapeutic alliance or to the progress of psychotherapy.

Ari

Ari's parents worried he would be expelled from school for explosive angry out-bursts. When he was upset at home, his mother often withdrew to another room while his anxious father looked to ease his discomfort immediately. Ari's school troubles improved during the first years in treatment although it puzzled me that I saw no trace of his explosive behaviors during our sessions. Mostly he told me about various aches and pains and how tired he was at every session. After a while, he talked about his fighting and shooting games on PlayStation 3 and X-box 360 but he never brought any games in. During one session, Ari was on the rug playing "pin ball" with a half full soda bottle. He wanted to see if he could put holes in the bottle label. Then he began to flip the bottle cap in my direction. Each time it got closer to landing on me, he would open his eyes and mouth wide in feigned surprise and mouth the word "sorry," but then with obvious pleasure continue to flip the bottle cap until it landed on me twice. While I was actually enjoying the fun Ari was having at my expense, I said maybe he was wondering how I'd react if the bottle cap hit me. When I added he seemed to be "teasing" me, he had an intense emotional reaction that I had never seen before. It began with a glum mood change followed by several minutes of tense silence and then visible shaking while holding on with both hands to the legs of a chair trying to control himself. Then he cried but was unable to say any thing more during the session other than that he wasn't teasing me.

Over the next several sessions, we talked about the meaning of "teasing." Ari told me again that he wasn't trying to tease me and he never understood that the word "teasing" could be used in a way that wasn't hurtful. He had learned from his Quaker school that "teasing" was no different from bullying. I thanked Ari for telling me this and told him I hadn't realized how he thought of the word "teasing." We talked about the trouble Ari had telling me what it was like when he had to control his feelings, especially when he felt misunderstood. And we gingerly returned to the different meanings each of us attributed to the bottle cap play. Despite the importance of electronic games to Ari, it was our therapeutic encounter around his bottle cap game that I imagine we will both remember.

David

David, a bright sixteen-year-old suffered bouts of depression and social withdrawal from school. He struggled with his mother who was convinced that his poor school performance was a direct result of his addiction to video games and the internet. Father agreed. After escalating arguments, threats, and groundings, Mother removed his computer cable when she caught him going online behind her back. In the midst of this battle, David shocked me and his family by an unusual self-disclosure. He acknowledged that he hated the idea that he was a man and couldn't stand going to school and facing people looking the way he did. That was a major reason for his using the internet and game playing. He found a site where he could meet people without having to relate to them in person. David was successfully logging in as a woman and found solace having people relate to him online this way. I mention this dramatic clinical example because it taught me that parent-child conflict over possible media addiction can sometimes hide deeper issues that neither the patient, family, nor therapist may be aware of for some time.

Lisa

Eight-year-old Lisa was having no success with her peer group at school. She wasn't picking up on social cues and talked too much, often telling stories she, but not others, thought were funny. Lisa's parents were very supportive of Lisa and raised the question of an Asperger's diagnosis at our first meeting.

Early in treatment, Lisa brought in her Nintendo DS or MP3 player with a kind of "Hey let me show you this—isn't it cool?" attitude. Then there were her WebKinz pets that she could interact with online, had their own minds, and could get sick or hungry. At some point, Lisa brought in her favorite stuffed rabbit, Kissy, which she set down on the table facing the two of us. "I brought it from home for company," she said. With Kissy watching us, Lisa allowed her imagination to play on the Legos and plastic animals as her interest in show-and-tell about animated figures and digital gadgets waned. Lisa talked about the kids in her class; some doing silly and looney things like clowning around all the time. She herself sounded like a broken record and repeated jokes she'd seen or heard. Then Lisa hit on the differences between what people say and what they really mean and how their actions don't always tell you what they really feel. As she talked, she created an elaborate caravan of animals carrying Lego blocks and she weaved imaginative stories about the Lion

King misusing his power, framing and banishing his brother, throwing his father off a cliff, and talking only to his royal advisor. As I watched Lisa's shift of attention from Webkinz to the less predictable and sometimes deceptive world of people, I wondered how much this change was helped by our relationship built in and around her transitional and imaginative space and the support of her parents. Of course there was Kissy's presence, too.

CONCLUSION

In conclusion, I have tried to elaborate on Dr. Cantor's chapter by bringing aspects of psychoanalytic developmental theory to bear on our concern with the effects of media technology on children's brains and behavior. My emphasis has been on the interference with human relatedness. I have suggested the importance for most children of critical experiences with loving caregivers who offer clarity of boundaries and support imagination and play. Meaningful face-to-face emotional exchanges are bed-rock for children to become a secure part of their human environment.

Chapter Four

Cyberspace, Transitional Space, and Adolescent Development

Christine C. Kieffer

The impact of cyberspace upon the ongoing construction of identity, subjectivity, and agency is thought by many to have been profound. Cyberspace immerses participants in a paradoxical experience of connection and disconnection in relation to self and other, a phenomenon which may be utilized both defensively and as a vehicle for creative expression. This chapter will examine the role of cyberspace in the lives of contemporary adolescents, with particular emphasis on the developmental hurdles of separation and individuation.

PSYCHOLOGICAL DEVELOPMENT IN THE ELECTRONIC AGE

While this contribution focuses upon the importance and meaning of cyberspace in the development of adolescents, it must be recognized that psychologists and other social scientists have been examining the impact of television on child development since the first tiny screens made their way into post World War II living rooms. Singer and Singer (2005) were among the first to empirically study the impact of television upon children, with particular emphasis on the effects of viewing violent scenes on aggression; however, important contributions also were made by Eron (1986), Huesmann (1986) and many others. One well-replicated set of findings was that repeated viewing of violent television shows, rather than serving a cathartic effect, serves as a model for later aggressive play—an effect which was shown to have a long-term impact on children's capacity for affective and behavioral regulation.

One other important question framed by these researchers was whether the relative passivity of television viewing might be changing private mental exploratory capacities over time, a question that has not been fully resolved and which continues to have implications for the use of computers. Implicit, observational, and interactive learning that takes place in the electronic age—as opposed to, say, reading books or listening to the radio—entails a different style and presentation of content, one which may require less imaginative involvement on the part of the learner. LaSpina (1998) found that the structure of textbooks for children (even adults) has gradually changed since the advent of the electronic age in the direction of featuring more pictures, shorter paragraphs, charts, even different fonts, which he believed creates a multi-sensory experience for the "user." However, LaSpina argued that this trend does not necessarily diminish the quality of the textbooks or decrease reading skills, but mimics the natural experience of learning in the natural environment in which there is complex stimulation. Moreover, as both LaSpina and Singer and Singer (2005) have pointed out, many young readers eventually tire of this form of presentation (a guidebook, really) and move on to more traditional reading materials. Children who were heavy viewers of television were found to be less imaginative that lighter viewers, who eventually transitioned to books. Left unanswered by these researchers, however, is whether—or to what extent—use of television and computers alters the structure of imagination and the process of thinking in children and adults, including the development of psychological capacities that lead to increased tolerance of frustration, abstraction, emotional relatedness, and self-reflection.

One thing is clear: the development of the capacity for imaginative and creative play in children provides a foundation for profound cognitive and personality development. While it is impossible to concisely convey the scope of research into this subject, it has become clear that different styles of play have different adaptive consequences. For example, Wolf and Grollman (1982) found that there were two basic styles of play with toys: children who are *patterners* tend to prefer playing with blocks, clay, and markers, in contrast to *dramatists* who prefer to dress up and play with less structured toys, creating various narratives. Singer and Singer (2005) have asserted that a combination of these two styles is likely to lead to the most optimal modes of thought.

Video game play and interactive kinds of play in cyberspace provide opportunities for both modes of play, although researchers and clinicians alike have wondered about whether these venues, since many are highly stylized, may foreclose upon imaginative play and thus curtail creativity. While infant researchers have demonstrated that the antecedents of interactive imaginative play occur in the earliest stages of life, most developmental psychologists agree that the narrative or experiential mode of thought begins in the three to five-year-old period. Singer and Singer (2005) have noted that "looking or listening alone without other sensory involvements can be misleading guides to action" (p. 113) in electronic media which become popular starting in this age group. They contrast the use of television watching and video games with the hands-on or sensory experiences of a toddler that are "critical in shaping a sense of reality that then can balance a fantasy world of storytelling or watching television" (p. 113). Neurologists and cognitive psychologists such as Wilson (1998), Luria (1932), and Vygotsky (1978) have suggested that the human capacity for conscious reflection, imagery, and fantasy depends upon children's experiences in the "real world." So, when a child with poor interpersonal skills reaches adolescence, builds a personal website, seeks friends in chat rooms, and, perhaps, has "cybersex" on porn sites or other virtual spaces, these experiences do not match the kinds of social-emotional learning that would occur during face-to-face contacts.

Moreover, some researchers who have studied children's use of computers, such as Provenzano (2003), have argued that new forms of social and cultural values might be in the process of being created through the use of simulation games such as "Sim City," and call for greater parent and teacher awareness and involvement in these activities. Adolescents and young adults may gravitate to sites such as "Second Life" (Boelstorff, 2008), a more sophisticated and "mature" interactive game, from which younger persons are excluded due to the nature of some of the activities that occur in this game. So, one question to ask is to what extent are such experiences the cyber equivalent of playing "dress-up" and trying on different roles, particularly since, in interactive games, one receives ongoing feedback from the other players? What role do missing implicit and sensory cues play? And what is the impact of such feedback if the other "players" are anonymous?

One of the scientific pioneers who research such questions is Sherry Turkle (1995; 2005), a clinical psychologist and professor at MIT, who has argued that a person's view of society and sense of personal identity might be altered in an enduring way by the complex and non-linear nature of cyber-interaction. She has maintained that those who play such games develop "a de-centered self that exists in many worlds and plays many roles at the same time . . . this parallelism encourages trying on-screen and off-screen lives with a surprising degree of equality" (1995, p. 14). That is, experiences on the Internet may be contrasted with playing different roles in different settings off-screen in which a unitary sense of self remains, although some would argue to the contrary, and I will take this up in a later section. Turkle stresses the role of "chance encounters" that characterize Internet interactions that seem random or de-centered, but whose patterns may be better captured by chaos theory. That is, complex events, whether on cyberspace or in "real life" may be said to have "emergent" properties in which new structures and organizations emerge from seemingly random events (Galatzer-Levy, 2002), stemming from increasing responsiveness to "strange attractors" (Harris, 2005).

While Turkle and Provenzano have stressed new experiences that overtake and dominate, child psychologists such as the Singers and others have noted that children and adolescents who start playing these games already have (including unconscious) inclinations towards playing certain kinds of fantasy roles, which mitigates the influence of the game media on development. Singer and Singer (2005) suggest that the hazards of cyberspace that are related to identity confusion or loneliness might be mitigated through adult guidance or even the availability of peer support, which is often more influential (in both positive and negative directions) with adolescents. Psychoanalysts have been beginning to report on their work with adults, children, and adolescents who have become obsessed with their Internet usage, demonstrating that clinical intervention can result in a resumption of development that had been hindered by these activities (Dini, in press; Gabbard, 2001, 2009; Galatzer-Levy, in press; Roth and Kohn, in press; Tessig, in press; Tylim, in press). This is a vast topic and I will be confining myself to examining the role of involvement in cyberspace upon the two major challenges that confront adolescents: a move towards relative autonomy from the family of origin and the related goal of constructing an adult identity.

Adolescence and young adulthood may be a time of life (so far, although as the current generation of young adults ages, this may change: an adolescent patient recently reported glumly to me that his father had "friended" him on MySpace!) in which the use of cyberspace becomes most important. While children's use of the Internet is frequently monitored, if not curtailed, and their use of cyberspace is most often limited to playing games, adolescents become able—and insistent upon—using many more forms, including cell phones, "smart phones," a wider range of games that may involve Internet participation with unknown players, and, of course, the use of social networks, which is rapidly becoming ubiquitous in the lives of teens and young adults. Since the two chief developmental goals of adolescence entail separating from early objects and forming new ties, as well as developing a more individuated and complex adult identity—in other words, separating and individuating—cyberspace allows this process to take place on a larger stage or "screen." Social networks such as Facebook, MySpace, and other communities allow adolescents (and others) to almost continuously construct and reconstruct their identities in ways that are, in turn, intersubjectively shaped by the larger community. Of course, parents as well as other authority figures are also free to monitor the activities of their charges online, sometimes to the mutual consternation of both groups. "Helicopter parents" may be apt to do this. In addition, young adults are becoming increasingly aware that potential employers may routinely scan social networks in an attempt to gain further insight into the character of job applicants. Thus, escape into cyberspace may hold for adolescents and young adults paradoxical elements of both increased autonomy and further enmeshment. But before addressing how cyberspace affects adolescent development, I would like to briefly review some of the processes of development that are unique to this phase of life.

ADOLESCENCE AS A DEVELOPMENTAL PHASE

Adolescence is a developmental period characterized by simultaneously forward and backward movement as teenagers strive to individuate from their early love objects and form a new identity that integrates the past with a new identity (identities) that enable the formation of new object ties and permit the attainment of life goals. Anna Freud (1936) was among the first psychoanalysts to acknowledge the importance of this stage of life, describing adolescence as a definable developmental phase heralded by the onset of puberty and leading to a renewed struggle to bolster a compromise formation between the ego and the id. While this "truce," first brought about in latency, gives way to a struggle newly fueled by physiological forces, the more firmly consolidated ego must now contend with superego conflicts as well. Anna Freud observed that adolescent upheaval is only an external indication of the many internal adjustments that are underway, noting that, while adolescent acting out of these conflicts receives more attention, neurotic symptoms may also result in withdrawal into excessive amounts of anxiety and inhibition. While adolescence recapitulates infantile strivings, adolescence may also be a time of unusual creativity, and it has been noted that many artists and scientists make their most important contributions in late adolescence and early adulthood.

Other psychoanalytic writers also have described adolescence as a time of re-working infantile conflicts, including Louis Kaplan (1984) who wrote of a "farewell to childhood" and Peter Blos (1962) who described adolescence as involving a second individuation process which can lead to firmer boundaries and greater stability of both self and object representations, with a resistance to shifts in cathexis. Of course, Margaret Mahler and her associates (1975) also have written about adolescence as offering a second opportunity to work through conflicts around separation and individuation. Psychoanalysts and social scientists—and, indeed, most casual observers—tend to view unpredictable and inconsistent development as one of the hallmarks of adolescence. Anna Freud (1958) maintained that the "upholding of a steady equilibrium during the adolescent process is in itself abnormal" (p. 164), since "adolescence is by its nature an interruption of peaceful growth" (p.164). (I often hear strains of Stravinsky's "Rite of Spring" whenever I read this passage). While psychoanalysts have tended to view development as a linear sequence in which previous steps must be filled in or worked through as scaffolding for later stages, writers who have applied chaos or non-linear dynamic systems models to explain growth, psychopathology, and therapeutic action have argued that these processes do not necessarily unfold in a predictable, preordained fashion (Galatzer-Levy, 2002; Harris, 2005; Piers, Muller and Brent, 2007; Seligman, 2005) and that this is particularly true for adolescence (Jaffe, 2000; Kieffer, 2007).

That is, chaos theory, which has become increasingly influential in the physical and social sciences, may be particularly useful in explaining the particularly uneven developmental process of adolescence. There now seems to be considerable agreement in both the psychoanalytic and psychotherapy literature that adolescence is particularly likely to unfold erratically, with often rapid oscillation between reflective thought and non-reflective action. However, over time, if all goes well, there is a gradual shift toward adaptation, with a movement towards an increased capacity for self-regulation, an internalized sense of agency as well as a more realistic set of goals and ideals (Kieffer, 2007). This is consistent with von Bertalanffy's (1968) principle of "equifinality," in which he demonstrated that all biological systems self-organize and self-regulate, with multiple paths towards a common developmental outcome. Systems organize around "attractor states," or "a momentarily stable, equilibrated place, a preferred topology or a particular behavioral mode" (Harris, 2005, p.85). Von Bertalanffy also argues that small changes in a system can lead to larger reorganizations, in which the introduction of a new variable (for example, an initiation of treatment and creation of a therapeutic alliance can be a new variable or "strange attractor") can create a fulcrum by which change occurs. That is, during times of transition (such as puberty) when sub-systems are not strongly cohesive (as is also typical when treatment begins), small perturbations in the system can have great influence.

Another systems principle that is relevant to development is that of "emergence," which refers to a situation of synergy that is more than the sum of its parts—one in which "something novel or surprising appears from a situation that is not even suggestive of this novelty—something arrives 'out of the blue'" (Galatzer-Levy, 2002). This seems particularly evocative of the adolescent period in which seemingly dormant periods can suddenly and unpredictably shift into periods of rapid change and growth. Emergence can be particularly useful in helping us to understand the process of play and creativity, elements which can be particularly salient in adolescence (Kieffer, 2010).

THE ADOLESCENT QUEST FOR AUTONOMY

Parents often complain that their adolescent sons and daughters have turned to video games and the Internet which almost seem designed to disconnect themselves from involvement in family life, and clinicians who treat adolescents have similarly noted their patients' adoption of cyberspace in the service of defenses against engagement (Galatzer-Levy, in press; Dini, 2008). However, as previously mentioned, contemporary parents may also make use of cyberspace in the interest of discouraging healthy moves towards independence. Journalists have coined the term "helicopter parents" to describe a kind of parent-child enmeshment, particularly when children go to college, with the electronic age providing many avenues for continuous connection.

Of course, the concept of autonomy, its very existence, and its desirability has been challenged by intersubjective theorists and self psychologists. Kohut (1971; 1977) maintained that the use of selfobject experience remains a feature of healthy adulthood and that selfobject responsiveness remains important throughout life. Intersubjective psychoanalysts such as Stolorow (2007) and Orange, Atwood, and Stolorow (1997) have deconstructed the idea of the autonomous self, maintaining the still radical notion that the self is continuously constructed within an intersubjectively constructed field of others.

Galatzer-Levy and Cohler (1993) also have challenged the importance of separation-individuation as a necessary phase of development, particularly for adolescents, and question whether this is even an attainable outcome. They further asserted that the view of conflict and turbulence as a hallmark of adolescence is the mistaken result of generalizing from a patient population, and believe that Mahler erroneously generalized from her own personal struggle in youth. Instead, they argue for an alternative developmental paradigm in which the end goal is the maintenance and elaboration of mutual interdependence. Their view also has considerable support from the field of psychoanalytic infant research, particularly among those who study the vicissitudes of attachment: Lyons-Ruth (2003) has argued for the normative aspects of secure *attachment*—as opposed to separation—in facilitating individuation, and Liotti (1995) has extended these concepts to clinical work with a patient population with severe psychopathology.

Some self psychologists have expanded selfobject theory to include a dimension of relative autonomy. There is a third "branch" of self psychology, in addition to Intersubjectivity theory, which has particular relevance to adolescence: Joseph Lichtenberg (Lichtenberg, Lachmann, and Fosshage, 2001), who developed his theory of basic and integrated Motivational Systems from his own empirical research with infants, while retaining Kohut's notion of autonomy as illusory, left more room in his theory for a consideration of such motivations as aversion/withdrawal and assertiveness/reactive aggression (as well as psychological regulation of physiological needs, sensual/erotic, and curiosity). Wolf (1988), while still considering himself a "classical" selfobject theorist, extended Kohut's triad of basic selfobject needs (mirror, idealizing, and twinship) to include adversarial selfobject needs (as well as a need for self-efficacy). Adversarial selfobject experiences entail a "need to experience the selfobject as a benignly opposing force who continues to be supportive and responsive while allowing or even encouraging one to be in active opposition and thus confirming at least partial autonomy; the need for the availability of a selfobject bond of assertive and adversarial confrontation vis-à-vis the selfobject without the loss of self-sustaining responsiveness from the selfobject" (p. 55). The origins of adversarial selfobject needs first appear in toddlerhood, and then become prominent again in adolescence as the teen becomes more aware of parental defects, accompanied by a de-idealization that is gradually replaced by a more realistic and nuanced appraisal in young adulthood. Wolf emphasizes the importance of a gradual rather than sudden and traumatic de-idealization as facilitating the adolescent's transition into adulthood, thus he incorporates a universal striving for autonomy into the Psychology of the Self.

Of course, Winnicott also stressed the influence of a facilitating environment throughout life, although he seemed at a loss when it came to adolescents (1965), stating essentially that one should simply keep them safe until this problematic stage ends. I will say more about his notion of "transitional space" in a later section of this paper. I have emphasized the developmental models over the conflict models here because every model of psychoanalytic development makes a place for adolescent striving for independence and self-direction.

ADOLESCENT IDENTITY

The second, related challenge for the adolescent lies in the striving to develop a mature identity, which is facilitated by the adolescent's more abstract capacity for play and creative use of transitional space. Blos (1967) noted that the "action language" of adolescence, while an important feature of the regressive processes engendered by puberty and its accompanying hormonal and cognitive restructuring, operates ultimately in the service of continued growth. He and others have observed that the adolescent often engages in "play-acting"—in various bodily self-presentations as well as in trying on different interpersonal modes of relating. This is the adolescent equivalent of play, in which experimentation with self and other, affect and cognition, illusion and reality may provide a second opportunity to re-work earlier conflicts and lead to a more adaptive and resilient adult identity.

The adolescent's locus of attention shifts from the family to the peer group, seeking new sources of admiration and emulation. Blos (1968) also has noted the adolescent attraction to the glorified images of sports figures and entertainment idols who present temporary role models. There is not infrequently a seeking of merger with the larger peer group—for example, the attraction to crowded dance floors, large musical arenas such as Woodstock and the "mosh pit"—in which they are watching a singer which serves as aids in what Blos (1967) has described as "ego states of quasimerger. . . . (which) . . . serve as safeguards against total merger with the infantile, internalized objects" (p. 175). Adolescents are attracted to various forms of group Internet participation, such social as networks (Facebook, MySpace) and alternative living spaces (SIMcity and Second Life) which offer both the experience of merger and identification with a large group, as well as the opportunity to try on different identities and modes of relating. (You may be interested to know that there are Second Life patients and therapists as well.)

Group therapists have harnessed these proclivities in the service of therapeutic action, noting that the peer group may exert considerably more influence upon adolescents than their adult analysts, and some have argued that group therapy is thus the treatment of choice for this age group (Pojman, 2009; Aronson and Scheidlinger, 2003; Azima and Richmond, 1989). (Recently, there has been an attempt to use psychoanalytic techniques in the service of training, e.g., online Tavistock study groups, as well as in providing support group experiences, such as twelve-step meetings, but there are obvious controversies in utilizing a medium in which identity can be falsified. On the other hand, those who utilize this approach have argued that cyberspace interaction serves as the ultimate "blank screen" (Roth and Kohn in press).

MULTIPLICITY OF IDENTITY AND A DISSOCIATIVE MODEL OF THE MIND

William James (1890) may have been among the first American psychologists to suggest that we are more aware of multiple self-presentations than of a unitary, "core" self, however, it was the French psychiatrist Janet (1925) who, in studying the *double conscience* of the hysterics he treated at Saltpetriere, developed the forerunner of a psychoanalytic conception of a dissociation model of the mind, with its implications for multiplicity of selves. While Freud and Breuer were initially influenced in their thinking about the mind by Janet, they quickly abandoned their belief in a "double-consciousness," adopting instead a unitary model of the mind, or "the unconscious," which has prevailed in psychoanalytic theory until more recently with the ascendance of the Relationalists. It should be remembered, however, that prior to the postmodern deconstruction of a unitary self, Fairbairn's model of psychopathology also included what Howell (2005) has described as "a broad category of attachment-based, or relationally derived, dissociation" (p. 12), in which a multiple sense of self is implied. Ferenczi (1949), whose work recently has been redeemed by Aron and Harris (1993), also described a process of self-splitting that occurs during a process of identification with the aggressor.

However, these preceding models of dissociation and multiplicity stress the pathological dimensions of these conditions, while in the past twenty-five years, a number of new (but closely related) psychoanalytic models—including Relational and Intersubjective ones spawned in part by the Interpersonalists—have stressed that a unitary notion of the self is an illusion—though perhaps a necessary illusion—one in which dissociation may better represent its chief mode of unconscious defensive functioning than that of repression. This perspective is bolstered by converging modes of scientific study, including that of neurophysiology, cognitive psychology, and early child development, all of which provide further evidence that mind, brain, and self constructs normally operate in multiples—that is, as a modular system, with each system displaying a high degree of autonomy. LeDoux (2002) has commented on "how fragile a patch job (the self) is" (p. 304), stressing that the self is nonlinear and non-unified in structure. Putnam (1997) has demonstrated that the self is first organized as a set of discrete behavioral states which grow increasingly linked over time, optimally leading to what may seem like seamless transitions. Siegel (1999) has stressed that "we have multiple and varied "selves," which are needed to carry out the many and diverse activities of our lives (p. 231). It should be underscored, however, that the acquisition of the capacity for modification and integration of self-state modulation is a highly social process from birth, in which the caretaker begins to help the infant regulate physiological states out of which affect regulation comes. That is, sharing of affect states is an integral aspect of infant-caretaker bonding, and as infants acquire increasing control over their affective and behavioral states with maturation, different selves can come to be activated through volition. Putnam (1997) maintains that this process is greatly enhanced by the development of what he calls the "authorial self," which appears between about two to four years of age. This authorial self is relatively *independent* of context and can, with increasing autonomy (if all goes well), activate and emphasize aspects of self that will promote coping and mastery. One very important expression of this function is the development of the capacity for *fantasy play*, in which children pretend to be different selves—rehearsing different roles and skills—which further facilitates an unlinking of the sense of self from a given context. I am stressing this capacity here because it may help us to understand how adolescents may be particularly apt to gravitate—and obtain a special value from—the forms of fantasy play that are afforded by the transitional space of cyberspace.

Sullivan (1953) viewed dissociation as central to the structure of the self, and his work foreshadowed multiple self theory, although he still thought of dissociated states as split off from a unitary self-system. Philip Bromberg, Donnel Stern, and Stephen Mitchell, all of whom were deeply influenced by Sullivan, nevertheless all have developed models of the mind that posit a more or less integrated set of multiple selves as forming the personality. Each self state is thoroughly relationally embedded and context-dependent, that is, will be mobilized in certain relational contexts (Mitchell, 1993). Mitchell (1991) cautioned, however, that to accept the notion of multiplicity of self-organizations "does not necessitate the abandonment of the distinction be-tween self-organizations that are shallow and conformistic and self-organiza-tions that have a long history and reflect deep affective commitments" (p. 22).

Bromberg (1998) stated that "a human being's ability to live a life with both authenticity and self-awareness depends on the presence of an ongoing dialectic between separateness and unity of one's self-states, allowing each self to function optimally, without foreclosing communication and negotia-tion between them" (p. 272). Thus, Bromberg views dissociation as a normal process, becoming pathological when it becomes excessive, or when there is a lack of communication between self-states. The most central properties of these self-states, however, are that they are discrete and discontinuous. For Bromberg, dissociation is not fragmentation, but rather a defense against it. He states that "consciousness becomes a cocoon unless it has access to vari-ous self-states that permit authentic engagement with the subjectivity of oth-ers" (p. 194), maintaining that the very nature of the "smoothness" of the cocoon is the basis of its facility in disrupting access to these self-states. Therapeutic action, according to Bromberg, involves helping the patient use the potential space of the analysis as a dialectic between his ability to pre-serve the self as it is, and to restructure split-off self-states into the personal-ity: "The patient's paramount need is to preserve the dissociative structure while surrendering it" (p. 199). Thus, Bromberg's theory acknowledges that the emergence of intrapsychic conflict is a developmental achievement.

Donnel Stern's (1997, 2009) theory of dissociation and multiple self-organization is a yet more fully constructivist model in which he takes up Winnicott's paradox about the given and the made: that is, Stern thinks of experience as a *dialectic* between the given and the made, although not always equal in their constituency, and describes the past as being as much a creation of the present as the present is a construction of the past. One of Stern's (1997) central ideas is that of "unformulated experience" in which he pays careful attention to the un-worded ways in which we encode experience. Stern defines "unformulated experience" as that "mentation characterized by lack of clarity and differentiation. (In the clinical encounter) . . . unformulated experience is the uninterpreted form of those raw materials of conscious, reflective experience that may eventually be assigned verbal interpretation and thereby brought into articulate form" (p. 37). That is, unformulated experience, as opposed to repressed material, has never been articulated clearly enough to allow for the application of traditional defensive operations, and this sort of material is typically first noticed through nonverbal procedures of interaction, particularly through the enacted dimension of the analytic encounter. More apropos to our topic today—that of the adolescents' use of the transitional space of cyberspace—Stern also explores the creative process, in which unformulated experience may be thought of as a form of "creative disorder" or possibility. While the familiar chaos of defensively dissociated experience is structured in the service of avoiding what may emerge, a state of creative disorder may be said to occur therapeutically when "quite literally, we do not know what we will think next" (p. 73). Reik (1951) also has noted that when an analytic session is going well, both participants are surprised by what occurs, an instance of what Galatzer-Levy (2002) has referred to in chaos theory terms as a state of "emergence." Stern's ideas also evoke Winnicott's (1971) notion of transitional space and evoke the potential space that is engendered when play occurs. Perhaps it is not surprising then, that adolescents are powerfully drawn towards the medium of cyberspace, as a playground that affords many opportunities to explore unformulated experience and permit creative disorder.

MULTIPLE SELVES AND CYBERSELVES

One key advantage for those who are drawn to opportunities to construct and play out new, sometimes multiple identities is the opportunity to do this in what seems to be a safe and pliable environment. Sherry Turkle (2005; 1995) is a leading contributor to thinking about how computers and cyberspace shape our social and psychological lives and she writes with particular insight and authority about how participation in this medium permits both a discovery of heretofore hidden aspects of the self as well as opportunities to explore and shape new identities. She has noted that Internet usage has provided considerable additional support for thinking about the self and identity as multiplicity as participants develop "multiple user identities" that tentatively permit them to explore novel ways of relating with others, both gaining access to previously dissociated self-states as well as creating additional channels for their expression and even integration. Turkle has also observed that, as other players relate to one's trial identity, the "user" is able to become more aware of aspects of the self in much the same way that anthropologists are better able to see their own culture in sharper relief by spending time in another country—that is, what Levi-Strauss (1963) has referred to as *depaysement.*

Turkle (2005) has thus been among the vanguard of social scientists who have studied, not only how people use computers, but also what the computer *does* to us, and this may be especially dramatic in the area of how it shapes our conception of personal and social identity. As Palfrey and Gasser (2008) have pointed out, while there may be greater freedom in constructing one's personal identity in virtual worlds, such as SIMcity and Second Life, it is more difficult to change aspects of one's social identity. That is, Palfrey and Gasser have noted that "in the digital age, a girl's social identity may be more fully and completely shaped by associations that are visible to onlookers at any moment through connections in social networks like MySpace, Facebook, Bebo or StudiVZ, or through links in her blog to the blogs of others. In turn, the actions of her friends can affect her identity and her reputation in ways that third parties can observe" (p. 19). Thus it is a paradox of life online that it actually results in a *decreased* ability to control one's social identity, and that, despite the greater freedom to experiment with multiple personal identities, participants may be more tied to (in the perceptions of others, and perhaps ultimately oneself) a unitary self than might even have been possible in earlier eras. These authors point out that someone might have been able to run away from a farm into the big city and create a whole new persona one-hundred years ago, however, in the cyber-age, this is much more difficult. (Don Draper could not have pulled off his reconfiguration of himself from a farm boy to a dashing "Mad Men" advertising executive so readily today!) Cass Sunstein (2009) has pointed out the disturbing persistence of online rumors that "go viral" and thus are more difficult to eradicate, citing the "Birther" movement's use of the Internet, who insist to this day that Barack Obama was not born in the United States despite the U.S. State Department having posted a copy of the president's birth certificate online. Stephen Hartman (2010) believes that the Internet may even have altered the nature of mourning, citing the existence of potentially eternal memorials.

Modification of personal identity and the maintenance of multiple identities—whether dissociated or integrated—may be easier, of course, in virtual worlds, which has led to the development of negative stereotypes of these spaces as "escapist," that is, avoiding the "real" world. Tom Boelstorff (2008), a cultural anthropologist who conducted a field study of Second Life, a multi-user domain (MUD) in which players have created an alternate universe, complete with cities, money, careers (there are even psychotherapists there!), and opportunities to create avatars—characters in which gender, body shape, and personality are developed (often enhanced)—found that many of the participants were not seeking to escape from their actual lives, even though participation afforded them opportunities to be something different. Boelstorff argued that "such negative views fail to consider forms of escapism in the actual world, from rituals to amusement parks to daydreaming: the degree to which an activity is 'escapist' is independent of whether it is virtual or actual" (p. 27).

Thus, it could be argued that these virtual worlds may constitute a form of transitional space in which participants have opportunities to play with identity, at a greater remove than would be possible in the family or in the actual community, but in a safe space that affords some autonomy—the irony being, as previously noted, that players may find their social identities circumscribed or co-opted by the field. Dini (2008) has noted that video game play may serve as a form of working through and mastery of unconscious conflict, observing that children and adolescents—and for that matter, adults—often engage in repetitive forms of play when they are working out a problem. Palfrey and Gasser (2008) maintain that online social networks can teach participants "what it means to be friends, to develop identities, to experiment with status and to interpret social cues" (p. 26). Wallace (1999) also has noted that online play can provide opportunities for role play and behavioral rehearsal that can lead to real and positive changes in personality and interpersonal functioning. Thus we can perhaps begin to understand the particularly compelling lure of the Internet for adolescents and young adults.

Perhaps there is yet another reason for its lure: the need for a global village. I often talk to parents—patients, neighbors, and friends—who marvel at their adolescents' rapt attention to the screen as they stay abreast of the moment-to-moment "doings" of their friends and popular heroes. What could be the allure of banal announcements concerning the itemization of what one just had for lunch, where one had just shopped, what one had bought and who had just "winked" (virtually, that is) at whom? Of course, most of us can empathize with the pain of having been publicly "de-friended" on Facebook and the narcissistic satisfaction of being able to count the number of one's social connections (and, of course, knowing that others see this, too). But most parents seem puzzled, if not disquieted, by the sight of their adolescent's face softly illuminated by the screen as they search for the latest updates, and as so many interactions with them are subtly (or overtly) interrupted by intermittent texting. (Texting while in the classroom is a growing problem, even for honors students). Perhaps these phenomena are signs that the "digital natives" are seeking to recreate a lost sense of community that has been eroded by modernity. I recently talked with a friend, comparing our respective childhoods in the Bronx and New Delhi, in which we were surrounded by extended family, friends, and neighbors in close proximity, and we wondered if the Internet generation might not be attempting to create the kind of virtual network that we had had available literally at our doorsteps, with abundant life going on in all of its tumult, vividness, and "multiplicity." While the journalist and social critic Maggie Jackson (2009) has recently issued a jeremiad about the Internet bringing about "an erosion of attention" and prophesying a new "dark age," it was clear to me in reminiscing with my friend that interpersonal life has always been fraught with distraction, and that one of the tasks of development involves learning to temporarily detach and focus (for example, to study) while also being able to reconnect and merge—with both serenity and excitement—in being part of the crowd (in my case, the crowd that snaked down Fordham Road and the small groups that gathered on the street to gossip, as well as amidst my family in a crowded apartment.) In the small village that was really my Bronx neighborhood, children and parents alike felt a sense of security and a certain sense of being "known"—for good and ill. (We didn't need Facebook—we had Mrs. Flaherty.) Adults would not hesitate to intervene if they saw a child misbehaving and neighbors, for the most part, were responsive. (Of course, there were the misanthropes and loners, who had their place as well—and who generally were tolerated). As Palfrey and Gasser (2008) and others have noted, one's social identity was rather firmly established and perhaps there were not as many opportunities to experiment with personal identity as in today's "culture." There were, of course, stultifying aspects of this culture that were a tradeoff for security. As Sartre (1944) put it, "Hell is other people." Could it be that, particularly for suburban, middle-class adolescents and young adults (whose lifestyle is, after all, a principal focus of all of these books on cyberspace, thus limiting their generalizability), in seeking to establish Internet connections in virtual worlds, they are creating for themselves a sort of quasi-village atmosphere that earlier generations just took for granted?

A FEW SHORT CLINICAL EXAMPLES

Most of my adolescent patients have been involved in cyberspace activities to one degree or another: texting, playing various kinds of games, using social networking sites, and sometimes getting involved in alternate universes. While, as a "digital immigrant" rather than a "digital native," I initially felt somewhat alarmed, particularly by these latter involvements, gradually I came to realize that my patients were attempting to use these activities as a form of transitional space. That is, my patients were using cyberspace in order to attain a sense of mastery over traumatic experiences and relieve anxiety, but also as a means of becoming more playful—with new identities and modes of relating to others. The net seemed like a safer place—a kind of learning laboratory or playground—compared with the more direct confrontations of their lives that do not always include an "Escape" button, the existence of cyber-stalkers notwithstanding. When invited to enter this space and work with them, I felt reassured that I was once again on familiar ground. While I have tended to work as an "armchair" participant, there have been some analysts who have played interactive video games with their patients, allowing them to grasp something essential about their patient's personality—which could then be explored interpretively (Dini, 2010).

Candace and Tiffany

Candace, a patient in her early teens, had been struggling to become accepted by her peers, yet had continued to remain on the periphery of junior high school life. While Candace had initially entered analysis blaming her autistic brother for ruining her life—specifically for messing up the house as he ransacked each room seeking papers to shred—so that she would be too embarrassed to invite friends over. It soon became evident, however, that my patient had no one to invite. One of the most searingly humiliating aspects of Candace's school day would occur at lunch time, when there was no place for her to sit in the dining hall. Eventually, one of the lunchroom monitors would escort her to that dreaded table of those whom Candace classified as "losers"—the Siberia of the lunchroom—where she would have to sit and eat, hunched over in shame. After some years of work together, Candace proudly declared that, since the start of high school, she now had some friends to eat lunch with—quickly adding that this was a *miracle* and that I had better NOT attempt to claim any credit for it. (I replied that, while it must indeed seem miraculous, I thought this change reflected the work that she herself had done in her analysis.) Later, feeling less defiant, Candace lamented that while she now had "associates" at school, she still longed for the feeling of true intimacy that she noticed the other girls seemed to attain so easily with one another. At times, Candace simply did not know what to say, and there would be awkward silences, soon filled by others. She still spent weekends alone. However, Candace then revealed that she found herself increasingly spending free time on the Internet, playing SIMcity. While initially occupied with furnishing her house (in a manner that was far more tasteful and opulent than the shabby house in which she actually lived), Candace soon began to make tentative forays into interacting with the other avatars on the screen. Of course, this also necessitated furnishing herself with her own avatar—an idealized version of herself, with stunning face and figure, and also with a "cool" style of interacting. Withdrawn from the quotidian drama of the high school where the stakes seemed so much higher, Candace, a bright and imaginative girl—who now took to calling herself Tiffany online—soon found herself developing a social ease that she had never before experienced. Tiffany displayed a notable flare for repartee, and could chat knowledgably and confidently with total strangers, winning them over with her wit and charm. For the first time, "Tiffany" found herself "popular" and sought after, with many friends and dates. Each evening, Candace could hardly wait to become Tiffany, leaving behind her tongue-tied ways and dull life, and becoming her much more glittering, confident persona.

Gradually, Candace and I noted that it was strange that, while she could readily interact in the sometimes tempestuous and conflict-laden milieu of cyberspace—after all, life in cyberspace in many ways imitated "real life"—she continued to feel constricted at school. Eventually, a sudden drop in Candace's grades led to her parents limiting her time online, and, at first, Candace was alternately irate and panicked by the thought of being doomed to return to what continued to be a relatively isolated existence. But as our work went on together, Candace eventually began to find herself becoming somewhat more Tiffany-like at school. By her mid-teens, my patient had developed a small circle of intimates as well as a core of associates, and even was beginning to attract the attention of boys—and she no longer was quite so absorbed in life on the screen.

Paula

Paula began her analysis with me while still in grade school. Adopted after having been raised in an atmosphere of neglect and abuse by birth parents who were drug addicts, Paula had been having difficulty in adjusting to life with new caretakers who, while loving, had instituted rules and structure, about which my patient had had decidedly mixed feelings. The early days of the analysis were characterized by sadomasochistic enactments that were structured around both "playing school" and later, in engaging in fantasy play that mimicked narratives of the Harry Potter book series. Eventually these kinds of engagements subsided as Paula worked through her complicated past, mourning both her lost parents as well as what might have been, disengaging from identifications from her abusive parents and forming new attachments and identifications with her adoptive parents and with me. As Paula entered her early teens there had remained in her character a strongly coercive and combative style of engagement that made for tempestuous relations with her peers (even more so than might be usual in this age period). While still in latency, Paula had had difficulty in establishing friendships (as had Candace), however, rather than withdrawing, Paula had been, for a time, a school-yard bully. (Attachment researchers have noted that young children who exhibit either insecure or disorganized patterns of attachment, sometimes later develop controlling, and often ineffectual, strategies for engagement (Fonagy, 2001), a form of changing passive into active). While eventually Paula relinquished this style of relating for more pro-social forms, her development of a more cooperative style had carried with it the sense of it having been more of a capitulation rather than the development of a quality of relating that was more firmly based in empathy and a sense of give-and-take and fair play. With the proliferation of cell phones and personal computers in her social set, Paula soon had a "taste of her own medicine" in the form of being bullied for a time by a group of girls who sent her taunting text messages. They had also developed an elaborate ruse in which they led Paula to believe that a boy upon whom she had a crush had been sending her ardent emails. This onslaught of cyber-bullying initially led to a retaliation that took the form of a brief but fierce cyber-war. While initially devastating to my patient, over time, particularly as she saw alliances shift and morph into new configurations, Paula emerged with a developing sense of how she might move on from the type of "doer and done-to" (Benjamin, 2004) relations that had characterized her family of origin and which still resided in her internal world.

What about a male adolescent?

While I do not have a cogent case example of a male adolescent to present here, I would like to briefly note a clinical paper that reports on adolescent boys' immersion in cyberspace. Some psychoanalysts have begun to study adolescent usage of online sexual materials, and are further starting to recognize the impact of culture on the normal development of desire (Toronto, 2009). Galatzer-Levy (2010) has described a form of compulsive masturbation with online pornography by adolescent males in which unconscious conflicts concerning sexuality and gender are defended against by conceptualizing them as merely the concomitants of physiological arousal. That is, he hypothesized that Internet pornography provides a particularly powerful means by which some adolescent boys are able to disguise the meaning of personal masturbation fantasies in the service of protecting themselves from the anxiety associated with the nature of these fantasies and their conflictual meaning. Laufer (1976) has observed that erotic fantasies—particularly the development of a central masturbation fantasy—play an important role in the development of a narrative of sexual activity that form the core of an individual's conscious erotic desires. Galatzer-Levy (2010) maintains that the availability and overwhelming stimulation of online pornography can hinder this transformative process, in part because it can obscure to the adolescent viewer the ownership of the manifest fantasy. This form of pornography usage involves "the effective creation of a B (beta)-screen in which fragmentary experiences of bodies, body parts and isolated sexual actions are used to overwhelm the functions of making meaning of erotic activity and thus to protect the adolescent who uses Internet pornography in this manner from the dangers associated with the awareness of personal meaning and personal responsibility for erotic (and often other) wishes" (in press). He would agree with Bion (1961) that B (beta)-elements may be used defensively and aggressively to interfere with their integration into a matrix of meaning. Galatzer-Levy (2010) demonstrated how the interpretive process helped his adolescent patients to own these aspects of the self.

DISCUSSION AND CONCLUSION

The literature on cyberspace as a medium for communication, social connection, and domain for psychological development has been steadily proliferating—almost exploding—with contributions, only some of which could be included here, from anthropology, philosophy, sociology, education, "technology," group dynamics, developmental, social and clinical psychology—and, of course, psychoanalysis. Bonnie Litowitz (personal communication), who is both a psychoanalyst and an expert in linguistics, has averred that "the tool changes the user, whether that tool is language, written systems, reading, or some other form of communication." Whether one disapproves or feels enthused, is made anxious by—or idealizes—cyberspace, it becomes clear that the "electrified mind" is here to stay, and that cyberspace seems to be changing the way in which we communicate, think, and maybe even feel, in both subtle and dramatic ways. This may be particularly true for adolescents and young adults. In fact, Todd Essig (in press) has pointed out that information technologies are now so fully integrated into the fabric of everyday life that the term "cyberspace" has become antiquated because it is impossible to "jack out" and he has justly criticized the psychoanalytic community for their continued resistance—even disavowal—maintaining that such a stance is a manifestation of a kind of organizational "death wish." Rather, Essig urges us to simply behave as psychoanalysts, and "attend carefully both to the personal and immediate unconscious meanings, motivations, processes and potentials, and to the specific features of the technologically-mediated simulation or enhancement being discussed" (in press). It is with this in mind that I would like to make my closing remarks and to raise some further questions for discussion, which I hope will be in the spirit of a book devoted to honoring the memory of Margaret Mahler.

In his book, *The Metaphysics of Virtual Reality,* Michael Heim (1993) urges us to make a "virtual reality check," observing the many paradoxes of cyberspace which simultaneously permit both increased proximity and distance from our most basic animal/human natures. If cyberspace supplants physical space, it also can provide a way of overcoming the anomie of modern life, as some of the adolescents described in this chapter seem to be doing. If, however, our most fundamental sense of individual and personal identity is somatically based, what does the incursion of cyberspace do to our sense of self? Isaac Tylim (in press) has written of the ways in which cyberspace extends the body as a kind of prosthetic device, pointing out that we automatically accept such prosthetics in the form of mechanical devices in the physical world. So we might consider the unconscious meanings of such devices and their relational implications.

Developmental researchers tell us that an infant's rudimentary sense of self first develops from the most basic bodily ministrations of his caretaker, and as well as the somatic and nonverbal interplay between them, a connection that undoubtedly includes smell, touch, and taste, echoing Freud's early assertion that "the ego is, first and foremost, a bodily ego" (1923, p. 26). If, as some of the more radical philosophers of the Internet, such as Philip Zhai (1998), maintain the distinction between "actual" reality and virtual reality is chiefly that we are coauthors of the latter, and if online communication is increasingly predicted to (virtually?!) replace the physical, what does this indicate about the qualities of attachment and interpersonal connection in the future? One is reminded uncomfortably of Harry Harlow's (1958) early studies of attachment, with the wire and cloth "mothers," and the tragic and lasting results of the monkeys who had to bond with the former sort of mother.

Zizek (2004), writing from his unique and provocative form of continental philosophy that is imbued with a Lacanian psychoanalytic perspective, maintains that "virtualization cancels the distance between a neighbor and a distant foreigner" (p. 802) to the extent that "the presence of the Other becomes unbearable" (p. 802). That is, rather than resulting in the "loss of the contact with a 'real,' flesh-and-blood other in cyberspace, in which all we encounter are digital phantoms: Our point is rather that cyberspace is not spectral enough" (p.803). Or rather that the problem with virtual reality is that it is too "Real." Galatzer-Levy's (in press) paper suggests that it might be this overintrusiveness of online pornographic images that assists his adolescent patients in their disavowal.

To those who maintain the distinction between the "real" and "virtual reality," couldn't one also reply that each person's sense of reality is virtual? Our internal worlds are virtual by definition, whether we think of them as co-constructed and embedded in an intersubjective matrix or as a production of a monadic mind. Perhaps it is our work with the digital natives—our child, adolescent, and young adult patients—that will help us to enlarge upon what Mahler has taught us about the nature of human development and connection.

Chapter Five

Cyberplay: The Pros and Cons of a "Macrosphere"

Monisha C. Akhtar

In early April 2008, from the sunshine state of Florida the following shocking story was reported: six teenagers, two boys and four girls, lured a young female peer to a home and proceeded to pulverize her face beyond recognition while at the same time putting it on YouTube. Their motive was simple: to teach her a lesson. The broadcast, they felt, would be so embarrassing as to socially castrate the young girl, making it difficult for her to function in their community. In another, recently reported local case, school authorities of the Lower Merion School District are faced with a lawsuit from a student who has accused the school authorities of violating his right to privacy. The actual incident involved a missing laptop, equipped with a tracking device, which was activated by the school when the laptop was reported missing. The device inadvertently taped what appeared to be a drug deal, though this has been strongly refuted by the student and his family. The authorities claim that the devise was installed to deter possible theft. The boy and his outraged family disagree. And then, we have the story of a young couple in South Korea whose addiction to raising an Internet baby led to the neglect of their real life infant, who eventually died.

These national, local, and international news items are examples of the complex, albeit dark, escalating role of the media today in our lives, raising numerous concerns and questions of the what, where, when, how, and why in the understanding of human behavior. For psychoanalysts, this is a virtual gold mine of conscious and unconscious motivation, though undeciphered, unabridged, and certainly inaccessible as we only have the news items to draw upon. Most analysts function within the confines of an office space where matters of theory (in this case of adolescent development) and technique actually come to bear on such topics. Though the impact of the Internet on the psychoanalytic process has triggered several thoughtful papers on the nature of transference, countertransference, etc., the paper by Dr. Christine Kieffer brings the dialogue to a larger forum for discussion. Her paper provides us with a rich and conceptual framework within which we can explore and expand on various ideas and I thank her for this stimulating contribution.

In her paper, Dr. Kieffer recognizes the complex and long relationship between media and expression of violence. As she points out, psychologists and sociologists have studied this association for decades with extensive documentation of its debilitating impact on affective and regulatory functions. Its influence on cognitive functions (though controversial and not quite substantiated), including issues of judgment, conduct, imagination, and an ability to think is also acknowledged. As she writes, "frustration, tolerance, emotional relatedness, and the self-reflective capacities are also affected," placing potential limitations on the capacity for creativity and imaginative play in children.

The vast implications of this line of exploration forces people to limit themselves to what they can examine and Dr. Kieffer chooses to examine the influence of cyberspace on the main developmental tasks facing the adolescent, namely the task of disengaging from the family of origin and the task of developing a more stable and congruent adult identity with a commitment to more adult-oriented tasks. The paper covers issues of theory and contemporary perspectives on adolescent development and also provides us with two clinical cases to illustrate how the Internet gets integrated into our clinical work. In my discussion, I will expand on four points related to theory and then look at some issues of technique.

ADOLESCENT PHASE AND IDENTITY

Adolescence is the time of significant biological, cognitive, and emotional changes for the latency age child who until then has hopefully remained sequestered, oblivious to the upheavals that are about to occur. Much has been written about this phase and certainly Dr. Kieffer's review of the psychoanalytic literature on adolescence covers many of the main contributions and controversies. I agree with Dr. Kieffer's proposition that today we cannot coerce all adolescent development into a linear progression wherein the individual emerges with a distinct self, going through a second individuation with the desired goals of emerging as a young adult, ready to take on adult responsibilities and participate within their social cultural milieu. When we talk about a social cultural milieu, however, I cannot help but think of Erik Erikson (1950) whose theory of psychosocial development captures well the integration of social cultural issues in the formation of identity. Erikson's eight stages of psychosocial development of which the adolescent phase is characterized by the identity versus identity confusion, provides an epigenetic viewpoint of the developmental ladder. Furthermore, Erikson, like others, recognizes that the outcome of young adult commitments depends largely on the outcome of the adolescent struggle for identity. He writes:

> Identity formation emerges as an evolving configuration—a configuration that gradually integrates constitutional given idiosyncratic libidinal needs, favored capacities, significant identifications, effective defenses, successful sublimation and consistent roles. All these, however, can only emerge from a mutual adaptation of individual potentials, technological world views and religious or political ideologies (p. 112).

I wonder how Dr. Kieffer would conceptualize the social cultural milieu of the Internet space, which is infinite, unstructured, and provides all kinds of information readily to the hungry consumer. Does this not constitute a social framework that often remains nameless, formless, and nonjudgmental? Having psychological space is good but having limitless psychological space may pose potential problems. A boundless space may have creative potentials, especially in situations of excessive anxiety tinged with guilt, but its possible detrimental effects cannot be ignored. Does this have an impact on the development of a social identity, which is integral to adolescent development? While Dr. Kieffer does acknowledge the importance of group membership, the issue of social identity, and the influence of the social arena afforded by the Internet, needs further exploration.

Dr. Kieffer captures well the current perspectives on the adolescent phase of development that have broadened our understanding of identity development and notion of the self. We live in complex times where the development of identity in addition to the emergence of mature adulthood commitments encompasses understanding of diverging ethnic, gender, and sexual explorations. The complexity of a cyberspace social cultural milieu necessitates a notion of multiple selves as well. It engages both theoreticians and clinicians to the plethora of possibilities that exist for young Internet surfers as they venture into cyberspace trying on different personas and giving free expression to multiple internal dialogues within the safety of relative cyberspace anonymity and disinhibition. The alteration of time and space affect group dynamics and John Suler (2002, 2004), a psychologist, has written a great deal about anonymity and appearance of disinhibition.

The notion of disinhibition also raises the question of whether the online identity is an expression of a true self. What exactly does this mean? Dr. Kieffer refers to this in one of her cases, where the online and offline identity were different but gradually merged over time. What is the relationship between the two and how and where does the Internet fit in? I will return to this point when I talk about Suler's theory of cyberspace and group behavior.

In reading Dr. Kieffer's paper, I was reminded of my work with a young adolescent boy who came to see me when he was nine years old. Our work over six years ended when he turned sixteen and as one can well imagine, I saw numerous cognitive, emotional, social, and physical capacities emerge over time. I think it is helpful when thinking of adolescent development that we consider issues related to early, middle, and late adolescence with each phase characterized by its own cognitive, social, and emotional state. This is relevant when we think of the impact of the media at different ages. For example, does the viewing of aggressive and sexual material at thirteen years have the same impact as viewing it when one is eighteen years old? Is one predictive of the other? Having said this, it is important to note that current online opportunities to explore different identities are easy, unregulated, and increasingly the norm. Valkenburg and her colleagues (2005) conducted a study in which they surveyed six hundred eighteen-year-olds in classroom settings and asked them if they had explored their identity using chat rooms and instant messaging. Fifty percent reported that they had explored identities and the most important motive was self-exploration (to investigate how others react), followed by social compensation (to overcome shyness), and then social facilitation (to facilitate relationship formation. If our psychological processes are similar online and offline, what exactly is going on when we hear of people projecting different parts of themselves into cyberspace? And when and how does it go awry?

John Suler (2004), a psychologist studying Internet behavior and group processes, offers another explanation for this phenomenon. He suggests that rather than thinking of disinhibition as revealing an underlying "true self" we can conceptualize it as a shift to a constellation within self structure, involving clusters of affect and cognition that differ from the in-person constellation (p. 321). He highlights six reasons why people extend their emotional expressions of the self while online.

- *Dissociative anonymity*: Individuals in this category experience an online and offline self as being different. The online self is perceived as alone and anonymous while the offline self is different and separate. Not usually seen as pathological, the other is often not felt as real.
- *Invisibility*: Simply put, it does not matter how you look when chatting with someone online.
- *Asynchronicity*: In this reason, the immediacy of a response is absent. According to Suler, this is a form of "hit and run"
- *Solipsistic introjection*: In this situation, the online companion now becomes a character within our intrapsychic world, defined by the online text description but also imbued with our expectations, wishes, and needs.

- *Dissociative imagination*: In this case, the characters created in cyber-space are viewed as belonging to a different space; one that ceases to exist once the computer is turned off.
- *Minimizing of status and authority*: The level playing field of cyberspace which masks the race, gender, sex, and other defining features of the online communicator contributes to a minimization of the role of authority which emerges in more face-to-face contact. This is freedom of communication.

Suler's approach to online behavior and self-expression provides additional information on what can happen when teenagers (and for that matter children and adults) surf the net.

CYBERPLAY

This then leads me to the second point and that is the one about cyberplay. I believe that one of the main thrusts of Dr. Kieffer's paper is her proposition that adolescents engage in cyberplay as a postmodern form of social posturing. In this process, they try on different roles and identities and express parts of themselves and explore hitherto unthought of fantasies and wishes. The relative safety of this transitional space affords the necessary degree of anonymity and freedom to ensure guilt-free playfulness.

The questions that arise from this notion of cyberplay are the following:

- Is the social learning that occurs from such play different from the face-to-face learning?
- Does this form of play limit the capacity for self-reflection?
- Does this venue curtail and limit other forms of imaginary play?
- Does this form of play draw a particular type of personality? If so, what remunerative effects does this have or how does this compound the task of adolescence itself?

Erik Erikson's (1950) remarks on the nature of play warrant mention at this point. He writes that "the original play theory of psychoanalysis was, in accord with its energy concepts, the 'cathartic' theory, according to which play had the function in childhood of working off pent-up-emotions and finding imaginary relief for past frustrations" (Erikson, 131). Another plausible explanation was that the child utilized the increasing mastery over toys for playful arrangements that permitted the illusion of also mastering some pressing life predicaments. For Freud (1920), play, above all, turned enforced passivity into imaginary activity. In accord with the developmental viewpoint, I at one time postulated an autosphere for play with the sensations of the body; a microsphere for toys; and a macrosphere for play with others. Of great help in clinical play was the observations that the microsphere of toys can seduce the child into an unguarded expression of dangerous wishes and themes that then arouse anxiety and lead to—most revealing—sudden play disruption, the counterpart in waking life of the anxiety dream. And indeed, if thus frightened or disappointed in the microsphere, the child may regress into the autosphere, daydreaming, thumb-sucking, masturbating. Developmentally, however, playfulness reaches into the macrosphere, that is the social arena shared with others, where it must be learned which playful intentions can be shared with others—and forced upon them. Here, soon, the great human invention of formal games, combining aggressive aims with rules of fairness, takes over. Play, then, is a good example of the way in which every major trend of epigenetic development continues to expand and develop throughout life.

In the light of Erikson's notions, let us ask whether the play, using cyberspace, allows for an epigenetic development, with the potential to master reality through experimentation and planning. In some cases, as in some video games, this might indeed be true. But I wonder how and when such forms of play goes awry when the transitional space of play is experienced as quite distinct from oneself and not as an extension of one's self and self-creation.

In 2001, a panel at the Division 39 meetings explored this very topic. Various speakers addressed issues of computer-mediated relationships, experimentation with different aspects of self via the Internet, and most importantly changes in children's play due to the new technology. A summary of the discussion held there (Hanlon, 2001) highlighted concerns about how electronic media changes the speed of communication, leading to overstimulation with enormous pieces of information, and undermine qualities of mind that have to with delay, lingering attention, and modulation of stimulation. One of the presenters, Prince, emphasized the privileging of virtual time and virtual space over real time and real space. Transformations in children's play is inevitable and of concern. Turkle, in this same panel discussion, introduced the idea that these children engaging in cyberspace play may not know what it is to lose something. This point comes to the forefront when we think of the new video game, manufactured by a Japanese company, that allows the player to engage in a video game of rape and assault. There are numerous such examples. In the end, the panel concludes that the new technology raises questions regarding the self, love, play, thinking, and the psychoanalytic treatment itself. These bear on today's discussion.

Dr. Kieffer (as do many child analysts) underscores the significance of play for an adolescent. She writes that establishing the transitional nature of cyberspace and its potential is imbued by feelings, wishes, desires, etc. of the participant player. Certainly, the so-called normal developmental progression of play suggests the gradual assimilation and accommodation of new and more complex schemas resulting in increasingly hierarchical organizational structures. While acknowledging that certain types of personalities will gravitate towards the Internet play, there is an absence of what actually happens in this transitional space. How does the player navigate, so to speak, this endless space, which alters one's notion of time and space?

CYBERSPACE AND AGGRESSION

I began my discussion by talking about the YouTube incident where a young girl being violently beaten was broadcasted in real time. I return to this as my third point. We are bombarded today by the damaging effects of the use of the Internet in instigating violence as well as eliciting passive voyeurism of violent acts. I wonder how Dr. Kieffer, especially as she reports a case on cyber bullying, thinks of the impact of this use of the Internet? Does this have implications for adult behavior as well? I am reminded here of Stanley Milgram's (1963) famous study in social psychology (I think everyone is familiar with this study). It had enormous implications for society at large and was a commentary on our moral conduct and equilibrium. I wonder if we are entering a new era of morality. A significant difference with the Milgram study is that in the case of the Internet, both aspects of intrapsychic functioning, the superego and the id as fused so to speak. While it is beyond the scope of this discussion to examine the development of morality, it is worth mentioning that the extraordinary access to all kinds of information via the Internet (as mentioned in cases of global distributing of violence and sexual messages) might raise concerns for the moral development of the adolescent. This is a sticky and tricky issue. Let me raise just two points in connection with this. Kohlberg (1981), whose name is closely associated with moral development, believed that judgment did not become moral until early adolescence (which of course would coincide with Piaget's (1937) stage of formal operations) but that moral conduct appears earlier. In addition, we cannot ignore Carol Gilligan's (1982) contributions along with others to the moral development in adolescent girls. I wonder how Dr. Kieffer might conceptualize this especially in light of one of her cases where the young girl engages in a form of cyber bullying. Even though it appeared to benefit the young girl (the fact that she was in treatment would undoubtedly have been helpful), I wonder if there are other troubling consequences, short and long term, to such an exchange.

THE PARADOX OF AUTONOMY AND ENMESHMENT

Dr. Kieffer points out, and quite rightly, the paradox of autonomy and en-meshment; this is my final point in theory. As she points out, "parents as well as other authority figures are also free to monitor the activities of their charges online, sometimes to the mutual consternation of both groups." Re-ferred to in the popular media as "helicopter parents, young adults are also so aware that potential employers may routinely scan social networks in an attempt to gain further insight into the character of the job applicants. Thus, escape into cyberspace may hold for adolescents and young adults paradoxi-cal elements of both increased autonomy and further enmeshment." This paradox does raise the question of whether these two seemingly contradicto-ry trends have implications at one level for more parental involvement (at both the level of engaging with their child as well as with the therapist) and at another level for the wish for more parental involvement. While the "helicop-ter parent" may be irksome to some, its ubiquitous presence in the world of technological tsunamis has profound implications for both child rearing and technique. I will explore this further when I discuss the clinical cases pro-vided in the paper.

TECHNICAL CONSIDERATIONS

I will now turn to the two clinical cases cited by Dr. Kieffer. Analysts are most interested in the engagement at the clinical level, where the impact of cyberspace can be felt most acutely or comes alive, so to speak. Who amongst us, working with young adults, has not experienced the inclusion of video games, cell phones, and even a laptop during the course of our analytic work, challenging the notion of analytic anonymity and neutrality, and ex-tending, perhaps, the play space of childhood and the latency years into the clinical setting. The inclusion of physical objects immediately introduces a point of consideration—the presence of the media itself in the analytic space. In the two cases reported, one gets the impression that the actual objects themselves were not brought in. I would like this point to be clarified and expanded upon by Dr. Kieffer. Now returning to the two girls—both used the net as a "transitional safe space" in which to explore new identities and modes of relating to others. At the outset, Dr. Kieffer informs us of three things. She introduces her method of working with teenagers. As she puts it, she tends to work as an "armchair" participant in contrast to some analysts who play video and interactive games with their patients. Both cases are of young teenage girls and Dr. Kieffer acknowledges that she does not have any male cases, though she does describe quite well the kind of gender-related issues that might be of concern. Both girls are struggling with what Erikson would describe as identity confusion. Developing age appropriate social skills though appears differently in each case. Let me elaborate on these three things a bit further.

Though Dr. Kieffer herself does not play video games or go on the Internet with her adolescent patients, it does raise the following question. Would the participation of the therapist in, so to speak, a hands-on way, with the patient, observing her online behavior, alter or impact the exchange in any way? Self-exploratory behaviors online can have disinhibitory effects (Suler, 2002) and this has been described earlier. Would the analyst's participation, even in an observational mode, alter the exchange, making it a co-created product? If we go that route, how would this participation be different from, let's say, playing a game with a younger child, say a board game or a dramatic enactment? Would the analyst's participation then, in some way, bring the play and allow the analytic dyad to work in displacement?

The second issue is the role of parents. Dr. Kieffer suggests in her first case that the young girl's dropping grades led to some parental sanctions on the use of the Internet. How was this negotiated? Did Dr. Kieffer have meetings with the parents and what was discussed? I think this directly addressed Dr. Kieffer's point about the paradoxical relationship between autonomy and enmeshment. For clinicians it introduces a dilemma. Though parent work has been espoused by some child analysts, like Jack and Kerry Kelly Novick, as quintessential in working with adolescents as well as, of course, with children, there are many who do not agree with this, fearing that it would jeopardize the therapeutic relationship negatively. In both case examples, Dr. Kieffer implies how the use of cyberspace ultimately affected peer relations. But it is not clear from her description how this actually occurred. Certainly, Candace who becomes Tiffany in cyberspace benefited from first projecting more mature and socially adept image of herself and then gradually adapting it to her real life. But how did this happen? How did Dr. Kieffer tie in these disparate experiences, online and offline, and when and how did Candace begin to shift over to integrating these different self-images and self-expressions in daily life? Furthermore, whom was she interacting with, as Tiffany?

In the second example, Dr. Kieffer describes how Paula's antisocial behaviors alienated her from others and hid her childhood history of abuse and neglect. From my understanding of the case, and of course it is hard to report all the nuances of a long history of working with a patient (Dr. Kieffer writes that in this case she began working with Paula when she was in grade school), it is unclear what Paula's relationship was with the Internet before becoming a victim to its attacks. Does Dr. Kieffer feel that being on the receiving end of cyberspace bullying is eventually what led to a more empathic stance on Paula's part? In the case of a male adolescent, Dr. Kieffer draws upon the work of others (Galatzer-Levy, 2010) who explored the relationship between cyberspace pornographic material and the development of desire in young adolescent boys. The defensive posturing of using online material presented solely as contributing to physiological arousal and to guard against issues of sexuality and gender. Though we do not always have access to patients of both genders, I wonder if the analytic process would have been different had the young boys worked with a female analyst. Does the gender of the analyst in this case facilitate the exploration of online sexual behaviors? Would this have emerged with a female analyst? There is also an interesting difference between the three cases. Both cases of girls center on issues of social relating and peer acceptance. Issues of sexual identity are only reported with the male case. I wonder if this in part refers to a gender difference in how boys and girls use online communication.

CONCLUSION

As analysts we are often preoccupied with pathology and perhaps since we see troubled teenagers in our office, our focus is on what has gone wrong and not always on what is right. So, before I end and leave everyone with the thought that cyberspace has a deleterious impact on the adolescent mind, leading to identity confusion, diminished frustration tolerance, and a propensity to increased violence and disinhibition, let me leave you with an encouraging research fact. In the area of social development, in support of Turkle's (1999, 2005) argument that multi-user games provide people an opportunity to experiment with different selves (an increasingly postmodern thinking of self), Subrahmanyam et al. (2004) conducted a study in which they analyzed a thirty-minute transcript from a teen chat room (fifty-two participants). These teens covered a wide range of topics from sports and sex to parental concerns, etc. He found that the participants discussed their feelings freely and when one expressed a particular concern, it elicited support from the others. He concluded that the Internet could provide a socially safe environment in which teenagers can discuss embarrassing topics and practice social relationships. Yes, it can be said that the Internet is indeed a strange animal, amorphous in structure, infinite in its content and potential and relentless in its pursuit of information and seduction of potential customers of any kind. The nature of the beast, however, is in its master. But when the beast shapes the master itself, we then have a co-constructed entity, whose epigenetic path in development remains largely unknown.

Chapter Six

Reality in Cyberspace: Patients' Use of the Internet and Ordinary Everyday Psychosis

Patricia L. Gibbs

I am going to discuss the role of excessive Internet use in patients engaged in psychoanalysis. Patients to be reviewed in this paper were in four times per week on-the-couch psychoanalysis. I believe that extensive clinical material will illustrate the impact of heavy Internet use on the transference and countertransference. The patients' reliance on omnipotent denial, projective identification, and autistic defenses will also be examined. I will conclude with a discussion of the process material that reveals the patients' resistance to transference work and preference for virtual reality.

PERSONALITY CHARACTERISTICS OF HEAVY INTERNET USERS

Review of the research indicates that overuse of the Internet/computer has been rising and now is seen by many as a major health problem comparable to other addictive behaviors, such as compulsive gambling. Research has begun to identify typical personality traits associated with Internet/computer overuse. Because some of these people bring their use of the Internet/computer into their analyses, these profiles are of interest, as they provide demographic and empirical evidence substantiating the impact of Internet/computer overuse, and contribute to a comprehensive understanding of these patients and their analytic treatment.

Chak (2004) found that shyness was predictive of Internet addiction among 722 young adult Internet users. Yuen and Lavin (2004) also found that low sensation seeking and loneliness were associated with Internet dependence in college students. His findings also supported shyness as being associated with Internet dependence. He discussed how Internet resources could be used to ameliorate shyness and foster dependence by negatively reinforcing shyness. Scealy, Phillips, and Stevenson (2002) also found shyness and anxiety to predict certain forms of Internet usage. Engelberg and Sjoberg (2004) used the Internet Addiction Scale to measure the extent that interpersonal skills, personality, and emotional intelligence were related to Internet usage in undergraduates. Results indicated heavy usage was related to loneliness and adherence to idiosyncratic or deviant values, and to emotional and social skills associated with low emotional intelligence, such as a poor balance between work and leisure. Nalwa and Anand (2003) also found loneliness to be associated with Internet addiction, and Whang, Lee, and Chang (2003) found that loneliness, depressed mood, compulsivity, and dysfunctional social behaviors, such as Internet use to "escape reality," were associated with heavy Internet use.

To summarize, then, shyness was found consistently to predict heavy Internet use. Loneliness, depressed mood, compulsivity, and dysfunctional social behaviors, such as the Internet being used to "escape reality," were all associated with heavy Internet use. This research is interesting in light of the schizoid and narcissistic features seen in the patients that I will discuss shortly. I will not focus on the addictive qualities of the Internet, nor seek to precisely define addictive Internet activity. Rather, I will understand Internet addiction here in the way that it shapes patients' clinical treatment. Heavy and addictive Internet use will be understood as reflecting patients' preoedipally organized dyadic transferences, and as the concretization of unconscious conflicts involved in the transformation of reality into virtual reality.

As I begin to present our first patient, Mr. N., we will see the development of a dyadic pre-oedipal transference, and also understand what Wrye and Welles in 1994 called the maternal erotic transference. Both of these kinds of transferences are based on a pre-oedipal, dyadic object relations capacity, which is unconsciously organized and repeated in the transference. Our understanding of object relations today, of course, is based on the seminal work of Margaret Mahler (Mahler, Pine, and Bergman, 1975; Mahler, 1968). Pre-oedipal and maternal erotic transferences reflect a lack of full self/object separation-individuation. The object relations capacities in pre-oedipally organized patients remain at least partially symbiotic. Mahler's work has been invaluable in understanding the types of patients that I will discuss—namely, those falling within the borderline spectrum of functioning (Kernberg, 1980; Mahler, 1971; Masterson, 1975).

The Case of Mr. N.

The material that will first be used to illustrate our discussion of reality, and virtual reality, is taken from an eight-year analysis with an unmarried man, started in his early twenties. Mr. N. was intellectually quite gifted and respected as both a student, and eventual professional. He was, however, plagued with a variety of psychosomatic illnesses, intense panic attacks, antagonistic and avoidant social patterns, and the inability to develop an emotionally and sexually intimate relationship with a woman. He lived at home with his parents, and saw them as being quite disturbed, hostile, and suspiciously reclusive. He used the Internet frequently since adolescence, and throughout his analysis. Mr N. commented on his Internet use, saying: "Looking back on it, I think I was kind of autistic as a child—I had an uncanny ability to entertain myself as a child, I would always play alone, for hours. My parents never liked me playing with anyone, especially girls. So I guess it makes sense that I would turn to the Internet—especially to see women."

As the analysis proceeded, Mr. N. developed an intense maternal erotic transference. Under the pressure of this transference, Mr. N. began skipping sessions in an attempt to control threatening feelings that emerged in the analysis. His use of the Internet, mainly to look at mildly pornographic pictures of beautiful women, persisted throughout this time, and throughout the analysis. After skipping his previous session, he reported a woman he liked had not shown up for class. He said: "I was sure she decided she didn't like me, or something. But I found out that it wasn't personal—actually, she was involved in a car accident . . . and you know, when I was driving back from class, after I decided not to come to the session, I was aware somehow that I was doing the same thing to you that she had done to me. And you might feel the same way I felt." He continued: "I felt . . . sad . . . I missed her, and I was worried. And it felt like she had taken all those negative feelings and just dumped them into me—and I have to say this—I was aware of this yesterday; that she rejected me, so I was going to reject you. And there was comfort in that somehow." I replied: "Yes. So one way to keep someone close to you is to identify with them?" He said: "That's right. So I did what she did. And you know—I do have feelings for this woman. She's been in my classes for a couple of years. And then I am afraid—how do I contain these feelings—that word containment—I keep thinking about it. I'm worried I won't be able to, and warmth will go over into love. I'm afraid she'll be able to tell—just through looking at my eyes—she'll see it in my eyes, that I have feelings for her. And so I can guarantee what will happen when I see her next week. I will be very cold and distant. I'm afraid I just won't be able to handle it."

Mr. N. would go home to spend hours on Internet sites, some being interactive, and most being mildly erotic or pornographic. He rarely dated and had had only two previous relationships with women, which were characterized by sexual difficulties, intense tumultuousness, and jealousy. He talked with difficulty about his Internet use, usually saying only that he "looked at pictures of beautiful women." During this time in the analysis, Mr. N. stopped paying his analytic bill in full for some months. This coincided with his statements that he felt "consumed by the analysis, and that everything was going into it." He also recalled in detail an intense romance of the past, saying: "When I had the panic attacks, I really thought I was going to die . . . the relationship was so consuming. It really felt like I was giving up my identity—that I would die! Basically what happened in that relationship is that I went away—left everything—lost everything, and was completely depressed. I thought about it yesterday—how I'm the one that is destroyed in a relationship. It always happens."

THE CONSTANTLY AVAILABLE ANALYST IN THE MATERNAL EROTIC TRANSFERENCE

Let's return now to a more precise understanding of pre-oedipal and maternal erotic transferences. Wrye and Welles (1994) have delineated the primitive features of psychological and bodily experiences of merger, boundary diffusion, and intense annihilation panic involved in what they call the maternal erotic transference. In Mr. N.'s material we saw his references to feeling consumed, which is organized by the pre-oedipal issues of fusion with the maternal object, erotic merger fantasies, and hostile fantasies of annihilation and death.

Wrye and Welles (1994) have also identified Shengold's (1985) developmental concepts of anal egocentricity and anal narcissism as particularly helpful in understanding the primitive features of the maternal erotic transference. The defensive processes associated with any psychic danger during the sadistic-anal phase amount to the ego's attempt to master overwhelming feelings ". . . by a kind of emotional sphincter action narrowing down the world to the controllable and predictable" (p. 71). The ego's attempt to master overwhelming feelings is associated with what they (Wrye and Welles, 1994) call "erotic terror." Erotic terror, they explain, can occur in both the analyst and the patient because of the primitive and regressive features of the pre-oedipally organized erotic transference.

LOSS OF REALITY INVOLVING THE PATIENT'S USE OF PROJECTION IDENTIFICATION

At this point, a brief description of my countertransference experiences associated with Mr. N. will clarify the loss of the sense of reality involved in his use of projective identification. As we will see, this loss was experienced not only by the patient, but also by me, based upon my unique way of containing Mr. N's projections in my countertransference responses. This temporary loss of the sense of reality has been described in the projective identification and enactment literatures (Boesky, 1982; Chused, 1991; Gibbs, 2004). I had been feeling "stupid" in the sessions with Mr. N., and also in my understanding of his material. I forgot the interpretations or interventions I made while writing process notes, and I became increasingly silent in the sessions, fearing I would say something inane. I feared I would be judged crazy and unanalytic, and would be prevented from advancing at my institute. I got lost *en route* to a psychoanalytic paper, and became so frazzled and anxious I simply left without attending it—fearing colleagues would be able to tell just by looking at me that I was losing it. Finally, I felt completely abandoned when Mr. N. failed to show up for sessions without calling—which he was now prone to do regularly. I had already identified my anger at Mr. N. for not having even the courtesy to call and cancel. In consultation on this case I further admitted, interestingly, that I now felt "abandoned—utterly abandoned—beyond rejected," in considering Mr. N skipping his sessions frequently.

At this time, I unexpectedly missed an appointment with Mr. N., and I was unable to contact him to inform him that I would have to cancel the appointment. I called him that night and apologized and explained. The next session, Mr. N. claimed he had no response to the missed session. After much silence, he eventually said: "Well, I know it's irrational, but I thought maybe you gave up on me. I felt completely abandoned." We went back to discussing why Mr. N. didn't call to cancel his many missed sessions, and he said: "Well, to be honest, I feel like I am just too negative. Like it makes me think of that woman—I feel she used me as a receptacle for all her negativity. And I think I am a very negative person."

As I listened to Mr. N., I finally became aware of a new way of understanding his skipping of his analytic sessions, and his failure to call and cancel. Much of his material at this time had obviously been a reflection of his erotic feelings for the woman in his classes, and for me in the transference. Initially, however, I could not see anything but hostility as the underlying unconscious motive for his frequent skipping of sessions. I had "forgotten" the beautiful women on the Internet that were there for him constantly, always waiting for him. Now I was able to say: "I'm thinking that your not calling me to cancel is related to trying to ensure that I won't abandon you . . . by not calling, you know that I will be here—the whole time—waiting for you, and thinking of your eventual arrival. I won't stop thinking of you for the whole hour." He responded: "Yes, I think deep down I know that you're obligated to wait for me. And I felt that same obligation—I waited for you in your office for forty minutes. And I tried to tell myself something must have come up, but by the time I got to the highway, I felt really abandoned." Shortly after this session, Mr. N. said: "I have this fear that I'm going crazy this week—that I'm losing my sanity. I think I've always feared that—that I'm unstable mentally . . . maybe I'll have a nervous breakdown. Today I was talking to some of the other students, and I really felt that they were better than me. I have that trouble—coming from my background. But I even felt inferior to them intellectually—which I don't really think is the case. My mind is racing—I wonder sometimes if the analysis will cause me to have a breakdown. Are you evil?" he asked. "In a way," he continued, "the analysis will result in a breakdown of my ways. That woman in my class—I had a nice talk with her today, but I was worried that maybe I was doing something inappropriate. I mean—we were just talking, and I know it sounds crazy, but I wondered if this other guy walking by was thinking that I was harassing her—last night I started to worry that I would be charged with harassing her!" I replied: "You're telling us that feelings of involvement and warmth are associated with your fear that you've done something inappropriate, and also involvement is associated with losing your intelligence, losing your mind . . . losing your analyst."

The Reality of the Analytic Method

A brief discussion of reality, as it informs analytic technique, is now in order. Keeping in mind the psychological and bodily experiences of merger and boundary diffusion associated with the maternal erotic transference, I believe that a consideration of reality within the "as if" nature of the transference must be done with an appreciation of the analyst's authoritative role in providing boundaries through the vehicle of interpretative technique. I agree with Gabbard's position that the analyst's disclosure of erotic countertransference reactions is quite untherapeutic (Gabbard, 1994). While there are those who argue that such self-disclosure to the patient is both analytic and therapeutic (Davies, 1994), I believe that this is not the case. I have found that postmodern concepts that insist that there is no actual, objective reality have limitations in terms of their application to analytic and psychotherapeutic technique. I believe that the analyst's maintenance of the analytic frame through an interpretative stance is the most powerful way to protect the patient and the analyst from the regressive experiences of "erotic terror"—namely, ego boundary dissolution, loss of reality, and boundary enactments.

Let's consider my final interpretation to Mr. N. at the end of the last portion of clinical material: "You're telling us that feelings of involvement and warmth are associated with your fear that you've done something inappropriate, and also involvement is associated with losing your intelligence, losing your mind . . . losing your analyst." My interpretation involved no disclosure of my previous experience of being disoriented at a professional meeting, and fearing that my colleagues would conclude I had lost it. I am not disputing the reality of those countertransference responses. What I would like to emphasize here in terms of technique is that self-disclosure of the analyst's countertransference only blurs the very boundaries and realities necessary for the patient to work through and benefit from the analysis of the erotic transference. Thomas Odgen (1989) states it is within the maintenance of this analytic stance that the patient is able to find what he calls the "father-in-mother" who will protect the patient from decompensation. Though Odgen (1994) sees the processes of projective identification as being profoundly interactive, his conclusion clarifies the importance of maintaining the analytic stance when he says: "Analyst and analysand are not engaged in a democratic process of mutual analysis" (pp. 93–94).

The above being said, I again agree with Welles and Wrye (1991) that in the case of the maternal erotic transference, the problem with most analysts "may be less of one behaving oneself than allowing oneself to participate" (p. 104). Dealing with these kinds of transferences can evoke erotic terror in both the analyst and the patient. Yet, if aggressive anality becomes woven into the very fabric of habitual ego and superego function, then the ability to experience desire and love will be seriously impaired (Shengold, 1985; Wrye and Welles, 1994). Working through and analyzing the pre-oedipal erotic transference may be the only way, then, that the ability to experience desire and love can be reclaimed.

The Analyst's Containment: Reality, Thinking, and Thought

An understanding of the precursors of thought, as described by Bion (1962), will provide a framework for understanding Mr. N.'s experience of reality, and virtual reality. Psychosomatic symptomatology, perceptual hallucinations, and action are considered to be the three developmental precursors to the individual's ability to truly have thoughts, and be able to think. In normal infant development, the primary caregivers contain the infant's projections of intense feelings. The child, of course, has no thoughts at this point, nor the ability to verbalize thought. In the course of development, separation-individuation may be impaired, resulting in object relations capacities remaining somewhat symbiotically organized. The adult in this case will then rely on these precursors of thought as a way to defend against unconscious conflicts threatening to emerge as overwhelming feelings (Arieti, 1974; Bion, 1962;

Edgcumbe, 1984). Sufficient containment allows these precursors to be mentalized, as Fonagy's research has shown us (Bion, 1962; Fonagy, 1998). Instead, unable to verbalize and contain his feelings of abandonment, erotic longing, and chaos, Mr. N.'s intense feelings were expressed as precursors of thought through the action of skipping sessions. Though the clinical material contained here does not reveal Mr. N.'s psychosomatic symptoms, these were also predominant throughout the analysis and used to contain threatening feelings.

During the analysis, Mr. N.'s reliance on the Internet served to partially contain his intense feelings involved in the maternal erotic transference. His projections of intolerable feelings of abandonment provided the basis of his experience of virtual reality. He transformed his unbearable projections into the beautiful women whom he experienced as never abandoning him, and always waiting for him. The hallucinatory aspect of Mr. N.'s "beautiful women waiting for him" is reflected in the transformation that occurred from reality into virtual reality and the reality of the transference: I became the beautiful woman waiting for him. It was essential, though, that I actually waited for him in reality, as the cognitive process that would allow him to verbalize his feelings of abandonment and erotic longing were not sufficient for some time. My actual waiting for him involved containing his projections until a verbal interpretation could be formulated by me, and then eventually be re-introjected by Mr. N. These intense projections were contained within the analytic stance, enough to allow several years of analytic work. We will return to Mr. N. shortly, but I will continue now with clinical material taken from the analysis of Ms. A.

The Case of Ms. A.

Ms. A. was in analysis with me for six years and in psychotherapy with me for a number of years previously. She was a never married professional woman of high intelligence, with one daughter from a man whom she knew briefly and never married. She was a tall, overweight, and stately woman in her sixties. Though Ms. A. progressed much in her ability to function without debilitating depression, she remained isolated and with few friends through much of her treatment. Her affect was often flat, and her associations filled with obsessive minute detail. She had been a difficult patient for me to see as the analytic work deepened, because of my continual sleepiness during her sessions. I understood my sleepiness as a reflection of her massive use of autistic defenses (La Farge, 1989; Ogden, 1995). My sleepiness was my response to her use of projective identification in which she attempted to shut me out, as well as her greedy attempts to suck me dry. We will visit a crisis in her analysis in which the computer is involved in Ms. A.'s struggle to experience reality in terms of her painful realization of my separateness.

Ms. A. never reported participating in Internet chat rooms, or using the Internet to establish contact with others—which underscores the degree to which she used autistic and schizoid defenses. She found her obsessive use of computer games to be an embarrassment, yet reported no success in stopping this activity. Shortly before making the shift to the use of the couch, the addictive quality of Ms. A.'s computer use intensified. She began to talk about missing work after staying up all night playing computer games. As the patient talked about being "entranced all night" with the computer games, and "not being able to stop," I understood that the computer games were a way of being unconsciously, consumingly, obsessively, and sexually united with me, the analyst/mother/computer in the transference. At this time the patient was being seen in three times per week face-to-face therapy. We were considering her adding a session and using the couch. At one point I said to her that it might be easier to talk about some things if she wasn't looking at me, with which she readily agreed. In the last session of the psychotherapy when she was still sitting up, I said: "Not looking at someone is easier for some people when they are talking about certain things . . . maybe sexual fantasies, or romantic fantasies. Could we say that telling us of staying up all night on the computer is related to wanting to tell us of fantasies of staying up all night with me?—Maybe sexual fantasies, or romantic fantasies—that would be hard, you tell us, to talk about while you are looking at me." She quietly said: "Yes, that's right, so should I lie down next time I come in?" And so the analysis began.

Being a relatively new and optimistic analyst, I assumed the magic of "official on-the-couch analysis" would quickly aid Ms. A.'s progression into whole object relations capacity, and a genuinely oedipally organized transference. Such was not to be the case. The analysis began, and continued for close to three years, with the patient being quite comfortable with using computer games as a way to be with her analyst. She insisted she found no need for close or intimate relationships with men or women, and would talk of masturbating prior to or after her computer use. Ms. A. did not object in any way to my occasional interpretations that her masturbation involved fantasies of being with me. I saw the computer as a vehicle for masturbatory sexual reverie associated with Ms. A.'s omnipotent denial of separateness. Ms. A. would confirm this by agreement, or further associations, as her material and affect remained obsessive, detached, and emotionally distant in the transference. I began to question the value of Ms. A.'s analysis, as I felt more depleted and lost in the merger transference and countertransference (Balint, 1969; Bion, 1957; Searles, 1979b). Ms. A. would have extreme difficulty talking towards the end of the sessions, and often had difficulty talking at all, uttering a few words, such as "Well, I . . . I . . . don't . . . uhm." Such utterances were paired with visible anxiety and even physical pain. She would periodically complain of a pain in her arm—which had never been medically explained despite frequent medical consults over the years. This type of verbal halting and fragmentation, along with somatization, is typical of pre-oedipally organized patients (Bion, 1957; Edgcumbe, 1984; Krystal, 1988; McDougall, 1989). Unconscious merger fantasies barred any communication between me and Ms. A.—as communication, of course, would involve Ms. A realizing that we were separate people. I defended against this massive regressive transference by becoming sleepier and more autistic myself in relation to Ms. A. At about this point, Ms. A. presented us with the following most curious outburst.

Ms. A.'s Reality on the Computer Screen

The patient arrived for her appointment, which had been her standing appointment time for several years. Interestingly, however, she arrived an hour late. I went out to the waiting room to close up for the day, and was surprised to hear Ms. A. coming into the building. I had assumed she missed her session because of a last-minute work commitment. Ms. A. looked at me and asked if I was ready to start the session. I said I thought she had missed the hour, as her appointment was for 5 o'clock. At this point Ms. A. flatly said: "My appointment time is 6 o'clock which it has been for years—as you well know." I began to feel that most unpleasant feeling of being drawn into something chaotic; however, trying to remain calm, I said: "Well, no, your appointment is at 5 o'clock." Ms. A. proceeded to angrily berate me, saying: "You don't have any idea what you're talking about! I've been coming here for years, and I think I should know when my own time is! There is no one else here now—I know it's my time. I drove all the way across town from work to come to my session—which I've done for years!" Ms. A. had followed me from my waiting room to my office (only a few feet) and stood angrily at the door, demanding her session. Knowing I could see her, as it was the end of my day, but would absolutely not do so, began to give way to self-doubts that perhaps I really had made a mistake—did I forget her appointment time? I began to wonder, and tried to visualize her name next to her appointment time in my book. I was scared not so much by her anger, but by the thought that I had perhaps so lost my bearings.

I said we could talk more about all of this tomorrow, at her usual session. Ms. A. left angrily, saying: "Well, yeah, we'll see about that!" The experience was momentarily unreal, and derealization would be the only word that could describe my countertransference experience of what had just happened. The moment I heard Ms. A. exit the building, I reached for my appointment book. With relief, I saw Ms. A.'s name next to 5 o'clock, though I couldn't really immediately believe what I saw. I read it over and over, and touched the page, as if somehow this would confirm my sense of the reality of Ms. A's 5 o'clock time. In Ms. A's next session, the following day, she came in, and sitting up on the couch, faced me and said, "Even when I was yelling at you, I kind of knew I had come at the wrong time. But I had to go back to my office to check, even though I had finished work for the day. My schedule was at work and I just wanted to see it on my computer." She said, "I just couldn't really believe it, though, that I could have gotten so turned around. So I drove all the way back to work, just so I could see it for myself."

What the patient was seeing was reality, and the computer was now an instrument to confirm reality, rather than deny it. Her previous denial of the manifest content of her mistaken appointment time, as well as the unconscious denial of my being a separate person, were finally becoming less necessary. The patient, for the first time in almost a decade of treatment, interacted, felt strong affect, and was related. Up to this point, she had never been angry at me because she had never before really experienced a "me" to be there—or to not be there—to forget, or not to forget, her time.

This incident occurred approximately three years prior to termination, and served as a turning point in the analysis. The anger mentioned above can be seen as the affective component of her capacity to separate from the analyst/mother in the transference. Anger, indeed, that her office computer confirmed, in reality—and not just virtual reality—that she was not always with me, nor I with her. Immediately following the previous session in which Ms. A. confirmed seeing the reality of her appointment time on her computer, she revealed a secret that she had kept in the analysis. Ms. A. explained that she had taken an antidepressant medication for one year, and had kept this from me. While she had used antidepressant medications usefully in the first years of her treatment, Ms. A. said she knew she was not any longer "really depressed." She said: "I knew you would see it that way, and I guess I didn't want—for some reason—for you to know." I said: "To know the reality, you tell us, that you're not as depressed as you were here years ago—didn't want us to see, perhaps, what we saw—you angrily leaving . . . leaving, coming back . . . really seeing things for yourself." She went on to say: "I know it sounds amazing, but I thought—what business is it of hers! It has nothing to do with the analysis."

In a way, I thought, Ms. A. was entirely right—it was finally her business. Ms. A's autistic defenses, and her omnipotent denial of the reality of separateness, had given way to seeing things in reality for herself. Towards the end of her planned termination, Ms. A.'s arm pain increased. She insisted that at times the pain was so intense that she could not lie down on the couch, and would instead sit up and face me. In response to her arm pain, I said: "Perhaps the pain is joining the analytic ending here—only you can really feel the pain in your arm, it's your arm." This led to the patient's realization that her body had never really felt like it was indeed hers, but rather her mother's. Being overweight became an attempt to differentiate from her mother. Decades later, her arm pain helped her to differentiate from the pre-oedipal computer/analyst. Psychosomatic reality and virtual reality had been transformed, and Ms. A. now saw reality on the computer screen.

SEXUALITY AND LOVE ON THE INTERNET

Some patients do attempt to use the Internet to meet others in Internet chat rooms. I'd like to now spend a few minutes speaking about how this kind of Internet use may effect psychoanalytic treatment. In all the patients I am considering, Internet use involved interaction with others, either virtual or real. Though these Internet relationships could evolve into complex and committed virtual relationships, those that remained virtual, without ever being consummated with actual real contact, had some essential features in common. These features might be summarized by a statement made by Dr. Ron Benson, a training analyst in Michigan. Dr. Benson states, and I am quoting him: "You cannot kill anyone, really, on the Internet, nor can you make love to anyone" (Benson, 2005). The dangerousness and sexual intimacy of actual real relationships, and interestingly, of the transference and countertransference, are missing in relationships confined to the virtual. Within the "as if" nature of the transference and countertransference, the feelings associated with murder and sexual intimacy are contained. The fact that these feelings could be actualized into real murder or sexual intimacy in the analytic session, and by definition never be so actualized in Internet virtual relationships, is worth noting.

Zizek (2004) considers the way reality, or the "Real," is altered in virtual reality, particularly in terms of cybersex. His description of cybersex has much in common with the pre-oedipal symbiotic object relations involved in the maternal erotic transference. Quoting him, he states:

> Virtualization cancels the distance between a neighbor and a distant foreigner . . . all are equal in their screen-presence . . . my cyberspace sexual partner is overpresent, bombarding me with the torrential flow of images and explicit statements of her (or his) most secret fantasies . . . when I am immersed in it, I, as it were, return to a symbiotic relationship with an Other in which the deluge of semblances seems to abolish the dimension of the Real (pp. 902–3).

I believe that in both processes—the transference/countertransference and Internet cybersex—there is something intrinsic within these processes that encourages regression. Reality is "as if" in both cases—with the one significant difference that the analyst and the patient really meet in reality, while also engaging in the "as if" nature of the transference and countertransference sense of timelessness. On this note, I would like to conclude by returning to the analysis of Mr. N.

Identification with the Hated Object: Mr. N.

As Mr. N.'s analysis proceeded, he made more references to increased activity on the Internet to look at "beautiful women." His skipping of his appointments without calling had evolved into chronic and extreme lateness, and became the new arena in which his sexual fantasies were played out and worked through in the transference. Arriving late, Mr. N. said: "Well, I guess I've hit rock bottom here—only ten minutes left of the session." "I wonder what is involved?" I asked. "The word animosity comes to mind," he answered. "If I antagonize you, you'll reject me, and that's always the way it is." I said, "And why would you want me to reject you—we've said because you are afraid to get involved, and that would prevent it—but I wonder if something else is going on right now." Mr. N. answered, "Well, then I won't have to tell you about my sexual fantasies." I replied, "I think you are telling us about your sexual fantasies right now—by being late, and feeling that you are antagonizing me—and that I am rejecting you—it's right here." "It's true," he said, "like with J.—it was very sadomasochistic. I would antagonize her, she would reject me—back and forth—until I went too far, and she finally broke up with me. So I wonder how far I can go with you here? It's like with J.—it adds to the excitement."

A sadomasochistic transference is always involved in the analytic treatment of a pre-oedipally organized patient. As part of this kind of transference, the patient struggles to contain enormous feelings of hate—both feelings of being hated by others, and feeling hateful, and sometimes murderously so (Gibbs, 2004, 2007a, 2007b). Identification with the hated object is inevitable in a pre-oedipally organized transference (Abraham, 1911; Bion, 1957; Lidz, 1989; May, 2001; Searles, 1979a). Mr. N. went on for the next year to slowly reveal his sexual fantasies, many of which involved being beaten or abused by a man as part of a struggle between the man and himself over a woman. Mr. N.'s sadomasochistic and hate-filled transference was associated with his reports of confusion about what he called his "attraction to evil." He said he found himself thinking about re-establishing contact with old friends that he knew were no good. This coincided with his confusion about whether or not I was good for him, as he would ask me "Are you evil?" and question the merit of the entire analysis. About two years after the previous clinical material, when Mr. N. again asked me "Are you evil?" I said, "Can we say there is a longing for your old friends?" He said, "Yes, that's right—and it would be the usual business—them betraying me, the whole thing. But I could be so close to my evil friends—you know? They would have destroyed me—they tried. Absolute evil." Mr. N. went on to say he believed his employees were rejecting him, saying, "Strangely, I take some comfort in that—it's like I like being rejected." He said he was usually sexually excited by being rejected—though there were times when he didn't feel he had to be rejected to feel sexually aroused, "like when [he] just looked at beautiful pictures of women on the Internet."

During this period of an intense sadomasochistic transference, after four years of analysis, Mr. N. said his mother had blasted him with her usual barrage of insults—telling him he was worthless, and would never amount to anything. This time, however, he said he responded in a completely new way: "I just calmly said to her—so, it's clear, what you are saying is that you hate me—so let's just make a long story short—you hate me, and I'm going to have to find a way to live with that—that my own mother hates me." Mr. N. said his mother was taken aback, and stopped her insults. After some silence, he said: "I might feel sad at some point, but I just feel I have more control now."

Ordinary Everyday Psychosis

I began to understand Mr. N.'s comment that he was able to feel sexually aroused without feeling rejected while looking at pictures on the Internet. Mr. N. was trying to avoid more active work in the erotic transference, knowing the enormous amount of hatred that he had had to contain over the years associated with his experience of women, and any kind of interpersonal closeness. "You can't kill anyone on the Internet, and you can't make love to anyone on the Internet" . . . that's virtual reality; however, the reality in Mr. N.'s transference, I believe, began to feel too real. Mr. N.'s sadomasochistic erotically tinged murderous rage increasingly felt too dangerous and real in the "as if" nature of the transference For years it had been safer to feel passively rejected and hated—by his mother, other women, and all people, than to feel his own enormous self-hatred. Mr. N. felt that he could not be rejected by the beautiful women on the Internet, but such rejection became an all too real possibility in the analysis. As Mr. N. became increasingly able to control his expression to his mother, and others, his hatred was directed into the transference, in the form of his nonpayment, lateness, and refusal to attend his sessions. Eventually, within this sadomasochistic transference, Mr. N. abruptly ended his analysis, I believe, feeling he was too dangerous to himself and to me in the reality of the transference and countertransference. For Mr. N., there was nothing more real, or dangerous, than the analysis when he left it.

There may be a very thin line between reality in the transference and countertransference, virtual reality, and the denial of reality. Reality is hard to define in terms of the transference and countertransference without an assumption that there is a reality that defines our analytic work, and that we can at least somewhat come to know this reality. The analytic method can provide protection from the chaos of the denial of this reality, but not always, nor perfectly. Though much successful analytic work was done with both patients, I have often wondered about Mr. N.'s abrupt departure from his analysis, during his sadomasochistic transference work.

I believe that the Internet, in the cases of Mr. N. and Ms. A., served to resist the reality of transference work and to express a concretization of unconscious conflict. I would further conclude that for these patients immersion and insistence upon virtual reality served the same function as a hallucination. As Arieti explains, in the hallucinatory process unconscious conflicts become transformed into perceptions, and the previously conflictual thought acquires the lower form of the hallucinatory perception. Hallucinations are one way that "concrete or close to perception form" (Arieti, 1974, p. 273) is given to disturbing unconscious conflict. Mr. N. had to experience me, in virtual reality and in the transference, as a beautiful woman waiting for him, in order to begin to verbally express and tolerate affectively his unconscious conflicts of abandonment, erotic longing, and murderous hate. Ms. A. also used computer games to deny the reality of her separateness, and create a symbiotic bond in the transference. Both patients' heavy Internet and computer use, then, served the same function that hallucinations always serve: namely to alter a too painful, hate-filled, or isolated reality, and to avoid the difficult work of separation and mourning.

Yet, the Internet also served the anxiety-reducing function of transforming the reality of painful unconscious conflicts and affects into a more bearable hallucinatory virtual reality. I would like to suggest that heavy use of the Internet and computer involved a retreat into an internal world of safety, (Steiner, 1993) in terms of what I call "an ordinary everyday psychosis." Because these "ordinary everyday psychoses" occurred within transference work, the hallucinatory aspects of the patients' insistence upon virtual reality also allowed for a transitional and containing function (Bion, 1957; Winnicott, 1945, 1951). In the case of Mr. N. and Ms. A.—and I would say all of us from time to time—this "ordinary everyday psychosis" affords us control over an otherwise too painful reality. For Mr. N., Internet use aided the transformation of virtual reality into a therapeutic "ordinary everyday psychosis" where productive analytic work could be done within an intensely pre-oedipal and sadomasochistic transference. Though Mr. N. had to deny his mother's psychotic rages against him for some time, his statement, "maybe I'll feel sad eventually, but for now I just feel I have more control," reflected his separation and slow dis-identification from the hated object in the maternal erotic transference. And indeed he did have more control in his relationship with his mother, and over his own depression. Mr. N. used the Internet to help make unsafe erotic and sadistic feelings feel safely real enough, even as the "as if" nature of his transference became too real and dangerous.

Chapter Seven

Preoedipal Paradise in the World of the Web

Frederick Fisher

Dr. Gibbs' presentation provides us with an opportunity to examine some crucial clinical issues in patients with significant preoedipal pathology who utilize the Internet as a transference displacement. In child analysis, the transference is often displaced to primary love objects still available to the child. In adolescent work, transference is often displaced to a newfound love interest. The adolescent may then suddenly request to terminate or at least make the analyst feel unloved and abandoned. In recent years, wiith both child and adult patients, interpreting the Internet as a transference displacement has become a challenging task.

The concept of preoedipal pathology often elicits unsettling associations to key words like arrest, deficit, merger, and regressive transference. Let us begin from a developmental perspective. Margaret S. Mahler, in 1952, described "infantile symbiotic psychosis" as a condition where the mental representation of the mother remains fixated or becomes regressively fused with the mental representation of the self. Starting as early as the second year of life, a perceived separation from this intrapsychic dyad presents as a cataclysmic event for the child. The child is responding not to the loss of an object, but to a loss of part of the self because self/object differentiation has not been accomplished. Defenses against the separation from the symbiotic object can include somatic delusions and hallucinations. Reality testing is significantly impaired. Anna Freud (1965) has commented that the child's sense of oneness with the mother's body parallels the mother's sense that the baby's body belongs to her, thereby establishing a crucial interplay between the two in terms of possessiveness and separateness. We can see this in the history of both Mr. N. and Ms. A.

Based on her extensive research of early child development, Mahler (1975) theorized that all children emerge from the symbiotic phase through separation and individuation. A partial but significant surrender of the fantasy of oneness results in resolution of the rapprochement crisis. While remnants of the fused self/maternal representation may persist, the child usually achieves a degree of selfhood around age three and one-half years and establishes what Mahler refers to as libidinal self/object constancy. With the self and object representation now internalized, the child can, with confidence, separate from the external maternal figure and feel safe. A recurrent fantasy of reemergence with the mother—especially in times of stress—as well as the dread of re-engulfment, may persist in some children even into early adulthood.

Clinicians see a spectrum of issues in separation-individuation pathology linked to the symbiotic phase. Stoller (1968) used the concept of symbiotic bliss to describe the wish of the male toddler to merge with the maternal figure. Subsequent research studies by Coates et al. (1991) suggest gender identity disorder as a compromise formation, with the boy conflicted over the wish to merge as well as the resulting terror over the loss of body integrity. Coates describes this process of merging as an "identification of being," a result of the failed resolution of the rapprochement crisis. In other words, in regard to the struggle over loss and restitution, if you can become someone, you never lose them. Recall Norman Bates in *Psycho* (Shamley Productions: directed by A. Hitchcock, 1960).

Separation anxiety generated by merger fantasies can manifest as school refusal, resistance to sleepovers, camp avoidance, and college withdrawal. Usually, reality testing remains intact until the individual perceives separation from the maternal figure, either intrapsychically or in reality, as danger.

While reading this paper, I thought of my patient Sally. Sally shared a bed with her mother. Upon awakening in the morning, mother would accompany Sally to her toileting activities, including wiping her. Mother then dressed her and accompanied Sally down the stairs lest she fall. Mother then served her creamy oatmeal because Sally had a history of difficulty eating solids. Sally then informed mother if she felt "well enough" to attend school that day. If she did not, mother and Sally would lie on the couch holding each other all morning watching television. Sally was ten years old.

Mother called me to evaluate Sally at the insistence of the school principal who was concerned about her record of absences. The parents felt that the answer to her school refusal was home schooling. Mother told me I would be "useless" because Sally would resist coming in and they would be unable to "force" her to meet me. I knew that mother could render me useless in their *folie à deux*. I met with the parents and offered to work with them, especially the mother, gingerly attempting to untangle the enmeshment to eventually reach Sally. Mother reluctantly agreed, but after a few sessions with her, I began to feel like a latter-day Rumpelstiltskin.

Sally became suspicious that mother was sharing family secrets with a stranger and demanded equal time. She insisted that she meet this Dr. Fisher because mother was telling the story all wrong. She told me later that she agreed to see me because she was afraid that I would remove mother from her life as if I were a surgeon who would remove part of her body. The evaluation helped me appreciate her paranoid world and the omnipotent stance she took to protect herself with mother as her essential ally.

Sally cautiously entered treatment. She was an intelligent, articulate ten-year-old who believed that she and mother existed in a timeless world as an amorphous dyad. Eating only non-solids and having mother wipe her and dress her confirmed Sally's belief that she could forever remain a child. Mother actualized her fantasies. Sally believed that mother had the exclusive ability to protect her from the threatening world and that only mother could make her perfect. Sally had difficulty separating mother's world from her own. At times, she was unsure whether an event happened to her or mother. She imitated mother's speech patterns, manner of dress, and mother's rage towards men. What value would a therapeutic alliance with me serve when mother offered her immortality? In my reveries about Sally, she would come into the office saying, "I want to go to overnight summer camp, and by the way, marry my father and kill my mother."

The reality of her pubescent state brought brief glimmers of interest in me as a man that were defended against by elevating me to the position of Supermom, a preoedipal action figure created to battle mother for first place. Sally gleefully watched us struggle. Oedipal material suddenly erupted in a sobbing confessional involving an intense preoccupation with Michael J. Fox. What strategy could I now employ to deal with my newly discovered competitor? She revealed that recently she had been obsessively watching his movies, usually in secret. She would become a famous singer and live an elaborate Hollywood life with Michael J. Fox as her protector. Rather than engage peers after school, she would run home and repetitively watch his movies. Between mother and Michael J. Fox vying for her intrapsychic attention, I felt useless and empty, sensing that my fantasy of rescue had unrealistic aspects. Could I compete only by entering the fused world of mother-Sally-Michael J. Fox?

Sally was tempted by mother's offer to avoid middle school by home-schooling and to spend the summer traveling with mom rather than a brief pre-teen tour with peers. After eight months of treatment, mother convinced father to stop therapy payments, yet they continued to bring her because they felt I had to be the one to reject Sally. Despite my awareness of their intent to sabotage treatment, I continued to work with her and the parents believing I would clarify the impact of the parents' course of action on Sally's future development. I terminated the analysis when I was finally able to appreciate how the power of my unrealistic rescue fantasy influenced my therapeutic judgment. For Sally, the promise of merger in her preoedipal paradise— bringing immortality, perfection, and protection—carried a price of loss of self that was replaced by a crude caricature of mother, a false-self.

In the analytic dance, each partner experiences a balance between the rhythm of the as-if, the virtual world of the transference/countertransference and the actual aspects of the rules of the game (schedule, payment). Lawrence Friedman (2005) captures the essence of this interaction in his paper "Flirting with the Virtual World." Patients like Sally, Mr. N. and Ms. A, who present a preoedipal, schizoid/paranoid picture, often limit the workable surface of the analysis, particularly when the transference reality is either displaced or denied.

THE CASE OF MR. N.

Like Sally, Mr. N. was enmeshed in a timeless preoedipal dyad. His brief but chilling history reminded me of one of Shengold's (1989) *Soul Murder* case reports. In his late twenties, still living at home, he presented more like a preadolescent consumed with computer porn. The parental edict of his childhood not to associate with girls continued into his adolescence and, then, into his analysis as a young adult.

I had the sense of Mr. N. as a possession of mother, not a person with his own aspirations or desires. Such mothers unconsciously offer the child the promise of themselves as an alternative to world involvement as long as the child remains innocent. To be sexual is a betrayal of their pact. For Mr. N., avoidance of women preserved his exclusivity with mother as well as protecting him from danger. In these situations, fathers often play a peripheral role in the life of the son. Often, with the onset of puberty, one falls from the garden of this pathological preoedipal paradise, needing to reconstruct a different world. At this phase of his development, however, Mr. N.'s drives were poorly modulated, object relations stunted, and the promise of the all-powerful mother became both irresistible and dreaded.

At a time when the adolescent begins a rehearsal for entrance into the adult world, Mr. N. began to retreat into the computer world, not as a transitional space to play, but as a retreat to avoid basic human interaction. Recall Dr. Kieffer's description of adolescents whose cyberspace involvement leaves them with unformulated experience. Dr. Gibbs reminds us that with the male, the maternal erotic transference, as described by Welles and Wrye (1991), represents a threatening merger fantasy that both excites and terrifies as erotic horror. In my work with males with significant preoedipal pathology, I found that heterosexual intimacy, even a hug, could threaten body integrity. If the relationship progresses, genital union, rather than being pleasurable, is perceived as destructive merger resulting in potential loss of body parts.

When I evaluated a schizoid twenty-three-year-old male college senior, he described a symbiotic relationship with his mother that included many enemas throughout his early years and latency. Recalling his first dance when he was thirteen, he avoided all contact with girls lest they excite him, saying, "They can take my erection away because they made it happen. It's safer if I'm alone." Although interested in women, he avoided intimacy because he feared that he would lose control of his anal sphincter and defecate. Dr. Gibbs mentions Shengold's (1985) concept of the anal sphincter as a container of affect/object control, and this young man avoided any involvement with women by demeaning them and being "tight-assed" with his money.

Mr. N. described his view of a relationship: "I was giving up my identity, that I would die." In erotic horror, described by Kumin (1985–86), the love object destroys the lover. The female vampire's teeth take blood; the lover's eyes take the soul. For Mr. N., women represented danger to be avoided or attacked. Mr. N. describes the threatening eyes of the young female student who interested him as well as those of Dr. Gibbs. The women on the flat screen, however, did not have threatening eyes, made no demands. Involvement with the computer created an altered, regressed state, where all things were possible in the virtual and nothing was possible in the actual. For Mr. N., his computer world provided an inadequate container for his affect and the illusory sense of omnipotent control.

Victor Tausk (1911) wrote *On the Influencing Machine,* a classic paper on the etiology of delusional thought patterns. He described patients who believed that the therapist constructed controlling machines that could influence their mind and body, especially the genitals. Today, individuals create, in their altered state, homegrown influencing machines, engaged in "as if" sexual or aggressive acts. In my work with several borderline male adolescents, the computer became a mocking, depriving instrument—the focus of paranoid ideation. In one situation, the computer screen was physically attacked, as it became the target of rage over feeling "frustrated, alone and controlled."

Amy Katan (1961) writes that verbalization provides the possibility for the ego to distinguish between wishes and fantasies on the one hand and reality on the other. Through verbalization the ego gains enhanced reality testing, secondary process, and regulatory function over the affects and drives. However, verbalization may not replace earlier patterns either of acting upon feelings impulsively or of projecting these feelings into others. In working with children, projective identification to communicate ideas or affect is often part of play therapy, regardless of the level of language achieved.

Dr. Gibbs' comment that immersion in virtual reality as resistance to transference work can be understood as serving the same function as hallucinations is described in Ferenczi's (1950) book *Stages in the Development of the Sense of Reality*. He theorizes that the newborn attains satisfaction by insistent wishing or imagining thereby ignoring unsatisfying reality. In so doing, the infant conceals needs through positive and negative hallucinations. In regard to the hallucinatory process in adults, Dr. Gibbs states, "The cognitive skills allowing conceptualization and verbalization of the conflictual thought have been somewhat lost."

Existence in Mr. N.'s contained computer world created a state of hallucinatory proportions where all things were possible. He avoided the analyst's words because he didn't want her reality to intrude. Better she should wait for him as he waited for his student. He was plagued by somatic symptoms or driven to impulsive action rather than utilizing reflection that would lead to thought as trial action. Patients with significant preoedipal pathology often present transferences that may be disorganized, primitive, fragmented, and difficult to treat with traditional analytic technique. The analyst may be drawn into a threatening countertransference struggle that parallels the patient's significant regression. In the case of Mr. N., the analyst, combining both the patient's and her own regressed state, sought to facilitate further work in the transference by untangling her contertransference reaction.

Chused (1991) states, "Enactments occur when an attempt to actualize a transference fantasy elicits a countertransference reaction (629)." Dr. Gibbs has provided a comprehensive report of the patient's erotic transference wish and the complexity of her resulting countertransference. She parallels the patient's affect and ideation, including her altered sense of reality that ultimately took the form of every candidate's academic horror—to be prevented from advancing in training. Dr. Gibbs missed an hour and was unable to contact the patient, a situation that caused Mr. N. to think he was abandoned but also, I suspect, that the analyst had retaliated in kind for his missed hour. The analyst linked the women who wait for him on the computer with the real woman who waited for him in the office. Mr. N.'s transference resistance had previously taken the form of keeping Dr. Gibbs waiting for him to invest in his analysis while, in the meantime, he was watching women on the Internet. This well-timed interpretation of his preference for a virtual existence permitted the work to deepen.

As a result of this work, Mr. N. requested increasing the analysis to five times a week. The transference heated up since, in his virtual world, the analytic dyad would spend part of the weekend together. He was then able to reveal themes of being physically punished in a triangular relationship. Stoller (1985) reports that aggression and humiliation play a significant role in the erotic imagination. Laufer (1976) informs us that the core masturbatory fantasy can be utilized to either augment or inhibit intimacy in late adolescence.

In the erotic transference Mr. N. describes being beaten by men when involved in triangular relationships. I speculate that "the men" represented Dr. Gibbs and that he could not reveal this to her or himself. In Freud's (1919) "A Child is Being Beaten," the sex of the aggressor can be disguised. This unspoken, and perhaps unconscious, wish put Mr. N. under great pressure, and he felt he had to act, not speak. In his mind, Dr. Gibbs was beating him and his paranoid defense was to retaliate. He missed sessions, avoided payment, and was silent. They reached an impasse and he fled. The premature termination of Mr. N.'s analysis may also be linked to his confrontation with mother and his attempt to free himself from his infantile tie to her. This encounter occurred soon after the frequency of sessions increased. Up to this point, mother was the third person in the room, watching and restricting him. I felt that his perception that she hated him was balanced by an emerging awareness that he also hated her. He then projected this all-consuming hatred onto every woman, especially mother/analyst. Since he no longer had to uphold mother's edict to avoid sexuality, remaining in the room with the analyst became overwhelming because mother was no longer a barrier between them.

THE CASE OF MS. A.

As I read Ms. A.'s material, I wondered what she wanted from the analyst. I had a nineteen-year-old college student who entered analysis because she feared that she would be unable to remain in college without mother's presence. One day she told me, "Tomorrow is my birthday." She had the fantasy that everyone she encountered would congratulate her even though she had not told them that it was her birthday. She was unaware of her motivation. When I asked her, "Who always knows the day of your birthday?" she uttered in a gasp of recognition, "My mother." She recalled that she often thought I knew things about her that she had never verbalized, and early in the analysis she formed an idealized transference towards me as the all-knowing mother. Why tell if I knew?

In contrast to Mr. N.'s dread of merger, Ms. A. merges with the analyst through vampire-like sucking, incorporating her desired aspects and utilizing autistic defenses to shut out perceived qualities of otherness. Tustin (1990) writes of autistic encapsulation defending against separateness. One can experience a spectrum of merging transference responses including "we are one," "we are doubles," "we are a twinship," "you are my imaginary com-

panion." Vivienne Lewin (2004) has written about the twin in the transference and references Bion's work with a non-twin patient who developed a
twinship defense to deny the separateness of the dyad. When Bion inter-
preted this defense, the work proceeded at a deeper level. Ms. A. had found
the all-powerful, all-knowing mother in Dr. Gibbs and used her as a symbiotic object, unable to accept their separateness, thereby denying the transference reality.

I was impressed by the compliant, little girl quality conveyed in the
material. I had the fantasy that Ms. A. wanted to refuel by snuggling next to
the analyst and experiencing the wonderful sensation of falling asleep together. The analyst was her best friend since she felt isolated, friendless. As a
good little girl, she was sexually abstinent. There were some naughty elements like staying up all night playing computer games and not doing her
homework, like paying bills. It was not clear exactly what Ms. A. was doing
on the Internet. She hesitated to make direct connections between her fantasy
life and the analyst. I wondered if Ms. A. finally acknowledged having
sexual fantasies about the analyst because, in part, the suggestion came from
such a powerful figure. Or, I wonder if this material was, in fact, homoerotic
and Ms. A. was unable to reveal such unacceptable behavior to her analytic
mother while sitting face-to-face.

Dr. Gibbs had the expectation that moving to the couch would magically
augment the analytic process towards an oedipally organized transference. It
is not uncommon for frequency of visits and duration of the analysis to be
mistaken for analytic process. Many candidates and seasoned analysts share
her wish, but she has the openness to report it. But did Ms. A. go to the couch
more out of compliance than conviction?

Ms. A. continued in a state of dual/unity slumber on the couch until the
mistaken hour situation occurred. The analyst, as the standard bearer of reality, awakened her and a remarkable shift occurred. Eventually Ms. A. was
able to perceive the analyst and herself as separate entities but only after her
computer schedule confirmed reality.

THE COMPUTER WORLD

We live in a society where there is the expectation of entitlement to unregulated, immediate, enduring gratification. The Internet can serve as a vehicle
of addiction for some to virtually satisfy their need to connect. Paradoxically,
the virtual highway creates both hyper-saturation and sensory deprivation.
For some people, the stage is set for an alteration of consciousness and a
habitual mode of non-relating.

The use of the Internet as augmenting transference was described by Glen Gabbard (2001) in Cyberpassion: "E-Rotic Transference on the Internet." An erotic transference was conveyed primarily through e-mail messages. The constant electronic communication denied the analyst/patient separateness and permitted the patient to assume a screen persona that enabled her to reveal an underlying forbidden incestuous relationship. Gabbard felt "the typing of e-mail messages created a transitional space for her in which she could play with new versions of herself" (735). Eventually, the use of the computer as a parameter was analyzed with a successful therapeutic outcome.

This 41st annual Margaret S. Mahler Symposium on Child Development is very timely in addressing the impact of technology on development, psychopathology, and treatment in children and adults. Today, we have considered the impact of our evolving electrified world and the role of the analyst at the interface of those changes. Dr. Gibbs has responded to the clinical challenge of working with two patients with preoedipal pathology, both of whom present with significant resistance by using the computer as transference displacement. Working with such patients in psychoanalysis requires a delicate balance between understanding their level of pathology and interpreting resistance presenting in the form of modern technology.

Chapter Eight

The Electronic Couch: Some Observations about Skype Treatment

Ralph Fishkin and Lana Fishkin

For the past two years, we have been enthusiastically involved in teaching, supervising, treating, and spreading the word about our work with English-speaking Chinese professionals under the auspices of the Chinese American Psychoanalytic Alliance (CAPA). We use Skype computer-to-computer protocols as the medium of communication. Colleagues have asked questions about many of aspects of our work, and these questions have stimulated us to think about the therapeutic processes and the personal aspects of our experiences. We would like to give an account of the history of this work, the technical aspects of setting up and proceeding, and some clinical illustrations that will address the many relevant questions that arise in the minds of the skeptical, apprehensive, and curious. We also want to address some thoughts about the similarities and differences of psychotherapy and psychoanalysis in the Skype setting, as compared to traditional office-based procedure.

HISTORY OF PSYCHOANALYTIC TREATMENT OF CHINESE PATIENTS VIA SKYPE

Elise Snyder, M.D., an American psychoanalyst, was invited to China in 2001 to deliver two papers on psychoanalysis at literary conferences in Beijing. She learned of a group of academics and clinicians in Chengdu, a city in central China, who were interested in psychoanalysis. She visited Chengdu where she lectured on psychoanalytic theory and technique, and provided numerous clinical consultations. She learned that there was a critical shortage of trained mental health professionals throughout China, primarily because almost no one was trained as a psychiatrist, psychologist, or counselor during the Cultural Revolution (1966–1978). The mentors and teachers who would have taught today's trainees after the reforms that followed this terrible period did not exist. Dr. Snyder returned to Chengdu a year later to provide additional training and consultation. Many members of this group, who were studying psychoanalysis in a non-clinical university program, asked to begin treatment with American analysts via Skype. A colleague of Dr. Snyder visited Chengdu shortly thereafter, evaluated a potential analysand in person, and agreed to conduct an analysis via Skype. This was CAPA's (Chinese American Psychoanalytic Alliance) first Internet analysis, begun in 2005.

Since that time, CAPA has been providing low cost psychoanalysis and psychodynamic psychotherapy via Skype to Chinese patients, primarily the mental health professionals who are involved in CAPA training programs. These treatments are conducted almost exclusively in English, and proficiency in spoken English is a requirement for acceptance. Patients are seen in analysis three to five times a week, or in psychodynamic psychotherapy one or two sessions a week. The analyst and the patient jointly determine the frequency of the sessions. What makes Skype so well suited for Internet therapy is that the computer-to-computer version is completely secure, thus ensuring the confidentiality of the treatment sessions. The computer communication, as well as the Skype telephone and chat communication, are encrypted on each computer and are changed with each transmission (Berson, 2010).

As of this writing, CAPA has arranged psychoanalytic treatment for over forty Chinese patients, and psychodynamic psychotherapy for almost thirty patients, all conducted on computers using the free Skype software. Psychoanalysts and psychodynamic psychotherapists are recruited from psychoanalytic institutes all over the United States. There are also several analysts from Canada, Australia, South America, and Israel. Clearly, geography is not a limiting factor. The major limiting factors are access to a high-speed Internet connection for both therapist and patient, a high-resolution camera and noise-canceling microphone, if they are not already standard equipment on the computers in use, and technical facility in the use of this equipment.

Chinese Skype patients are mostly mental health professionals with varying levels of experience. They are in training in the CAPA psychodynamic psychotherapy program, also conducted on Skype. CAPA strongly recommends that, just as in American psychoanalytic and psychotherapeutic educational programs, students undertake personal treatment. Many of the Chinese students who apply to the low fee CAPA treatment program are screened for suitability for analysis or psychotherapy, and are referred to an analyst or psychotherapist for further evaluation. If accepted, a therapeutic contract is made between the therapist and the patient, and treatment is begun.

The parameters of treatment via Skype are not significantly different from those in a face-to-face setting. If anything, Chinese patients are even more highly motivated than their American counterparts, because they are aware of how fortunate they are to be selected to participate in the CAPA program. Alternatives for treatment in China are few, and these are not uniformly at a level of competence that we would find acceptable. Thus, the premature termination rate, both among therapists and patients, has been low. The feedback from CAPA analysts is mostly positive. They have found this opportunity to work with patients from a country and culture vastly different from theirs to be challenging, stimulating, and gratifying. The technological hurdles have not proved to be insurmountable.

CLINICAL ILLUSTRATIONS

Ms. A. (Patient of Dr. Lana Fishkin)

The patient, Ms. A., was a thirty-four-year-old married graduate student, attending one of the most prestigious universities in China. She had been a PhD candidate for several years, majoring in an engineering field. She had approached Dr. Elise Snyder, the American president of CAPA, after having attended her lecture about psychoanalysis given at this womEn's university. Ms. A. was intrigued by this approach to exploring psychological conflicts, and requested an evaluation for possible psychoanalytic treatment. She was referred to me for an assessment, which was conducted over the Internet, via Skype. Although her English was sometimes halting, she was open and articulate, and provided a comprehensive personal history that was adequate for a determination of her analyzability.

Ms. A. belongs to the first generation of only children, as her parents adhered to the stringent Chinese government policy, implemented in 1979, for population control. She had always felt the pressure of their hopes and expectations, all intensely focused upon her alone (Fong, 2007). The parents, now in their sixties, were retired and living in another city. The father had worked far away in another city for the first four years of the patient's life. She lived during that time with her mother, a factory worker, and her maternal grandmother, who cared for her while her mother worked. Significantly, Ms. A. spontaneously commented that the Chinese people have great difficulty expressing their positive feelings, and that her parents never told her that they loved her and were proud of her, although she knew that they were. Instead, they were chronically critical of her, always expecting her to do better. She characterized her parents as "emotionally abusive," frequently creating feelings of shame and anger within her.

Nevertheless, her need to be "number one" was reenacted over and over in her academic and professional life, often complicating her relationships with others. Ms. A. provided little information about her husband of eight years or about her small daughter, both of whom remained in her hometown city, with her parents, while she pursued her graduate studies for several of those years. She and her husband were both students at their university when they met and fell in love. They continued to be "very close," speaking every night, and spending long weekends together each month so that the family could be together. The husband was a college professor who taught medical students in a university in their hometown, while Ms. A.'s mother took care of their daughter, their only child as per government policy.

Ms. A. indicated that she had significant conflicts about her aggressive impulses, a strong need for approval, especially from those in authority, and difficulty in saying "no." She experienced a great deal of anxiety in situations where her inclination was to do otherwise. She was eager to begin psychoanalytic treatment, and a therapeutic contract was established. The assessment sessions were conducted face-to-face, or, more accurately, computer-to-computer. The analytic sessions commenced with the patient continuing to view me on her computer monitor. After several months, I asked my patient about taking a more "analytic" position (although there certainly is divided opinion as to whether the couch is required for the proper conduct of an analysis) (Schachter and Kachele, in press). She moved to her bed, rotating her computer monitor to face the bed upon which she lay, so that my view of her was exactly as it would be of a patient lying on the analytic couch in my office. She was instructed to say everything that came to mind. She spoke freely during each session, within the confines of her sometimes halting, and occasionally idiosyncratic, English. I rarely had difficulty understanding her. Sometimes it was easier to comprehend the "sense" of the narrative than to fix on each word. I carefully chose the wording of my interventions, to avoid American slang or jargon. For example, when she proudly described a clever solution to a problem that had interfered with her professional advancement, I was about to comment, "There is more than one way to skin a cat," when I realized that the literal meaning of this common saying is grisly, and so found a different response!

Ms. A. talked at length about her difficulty expressing her feelings, especially angry ones. She could readily see that this was related to her need to be universally liked and admired. Her conflict was reinforced, she remarked, by the Chinese cultural value of "equanimity," requiring the suppression of strong feelings. Other feelings that have been conspicuous by their absence in our sessions are sexual feelings. I have felt some reluctance to point this out, as it is not clear to me to what extent this omission is cultural and how much is inhibition.

An early dream that Ms. A. reported indicated her conflicts about professional advancement at the expense of her family. The dream portrayed her wish to forge ahead, carving out a burgeoning career in her adopted city, as well as her guilt about uprooting her family, including parents who are her sole responsibility, in order to relocate them all to this city. She struggled with feelings of selfishness: returning to her hometown would put her back to "zero" professionally, as she now had many contacts where she currently worked.

Over the course of several years, Ms. A. developed a very positive transference to me, she frequently referred to me as her "psychological grandmother," explaining that she always felt encouragement, support, and unconditional love from her maternal grandmother, who lived with the family and took care of her. Her grandmother died when the patient was a preadolescent—a devastating loss. Ms. A. remarked that she felt so "relaxed" during our analytic sessions, that she could tell me anything without concern that I would be critical or disapproving.

After the analysis had been in progress for almost two years, I had an opportunity to meet Ms. A. in China when I participated in a CAPA program visiting five major Chinese cities and doing consultations and teaching. I visited the city where my patient lived. It was difficult to contain my excitement and sense of anticipation! We arranged to meet in a private room in a teahouse adjacent to my hotel. For the price of a pot of tea, we had a completely soundproof, comfortable private room, tastefully furnished with two facing leather couches. We conducted a somewhat extended analytic session, not unlike our regular Skype sessions. I asked her how she felt about meeting me in person. Her response was both surprising and reassuring. She commented that, although she was delighted to meet me, it didn't seem all that different from our Skype sessions. On Skype, she felt able to discuss anything that occurred to her, and being with me in that teahouse felt very familiar. She said that she felt "totally comfortable" with me, and grateful that she had the opportunity to undertake an analysis. I finished my tea, and we concluded our session. Upon my return from China, two weeks later, we resumed our Skype sessions uneventfully.

During the course of the analysis, Ms. A. has explored her transferential relationship to a mentor who was initially idealized, subsequently devalued, and more recently has become a more reality-based figure, important and helpful to the patient's professional development, but clearly with limitations and deficiencies. Her feelings about this professor have paralleled those concerning her father, about whom she has similarly come to a more accepting understanding. Ms. A. related a recurrent anxiety dream, which had troubled her since middle school: she was taking exams in physics and chemistry, and had somehow failed to study for them adequately. She always awoke from this dream feeling anxious and unprepared. Her associations were that these sciences were always difficult subjects for her, and created much distress. However, in a recent version of this dream, she was able to reassure herself, that she still had time to study, that she didn't have to get As, and that she just had to pass. She awoke feeling calm!

Recently there have been some hints of negative transference toward me, amid the glowingly positive "grandmother" transference that has been constant. There were a number of cancelled sessions, initiated by each of us, due to conferences, illnesses, and vacations. Ms. A. admitted, with great difficulty, that she was surprised to notice that she felt relief when we cancelled, as she was running out of "problems" to bring to the analysis. Such feelings made her feel extremely guilty, thinking that I would be "disappointed" to hear this. I suggested that the treatment was becoming less important, as many conflicts had been resolved. Ms. A. commented that she had more self-confidence, could express negative feelings more easily, and was much more effective in her interpersonal dealings. She was looking forward to the impending move of her family, including her parents, to her adopted city, where her husband had accepted a teaching position. Given the unique conditions of this analysis, in that I have been treating someone thousands of miles from my office, someone from a different culture, and whose native language is not English, I have been reassured by the familiar unfolding of the analytic process. It has been much like what I have experienced with patients physically in my office. The reach of the Internet and the opportunities that it provides are nothing short of miraculous.

Mr. B. (Patient of Dr. Ralph Fishkin)

The patient, Mr. B., is a forty-year-old married male psychology graduate student in a large Chinese city. He and his wife are both ambitious professionals who have chosen not to have children. He spent several years in London as a graduate student in another field, and his English is fluent and spoken distinctly, with a slight British accent. Mr. B. was an MBA who had a consulting business, but found the work trivial and became disenchanted with his career. He thought he could find satisfaction as a clinical psychologist and had begun to read about theories of psychology. He then applied and was accepted to a psychology graduate program leading, ultimately, to a doctoral degree. Concomitant with his graduate work, he took "trainings," very common in China, in a number of clinical specialties, including transactional analysis, a variety of family therapy systems, and Jungian and Freudian psychoanalysis. Various Western authorities give these "trainings." Typically, they come to China to teach for a week or so at a time, two or three times during the year. A colleague told him about the CAPA program, whose course work and supervision extend throughout the year, and he enrolled because the immersion appealed to him.

He became interested in psychoanalytic treatment during his first year in the CAPA program, as he became aware of angry feelings stirred up in him by certain of his patients, feelings that he didn't understand, but which he knew would limit his effectiveness and undermine his intense motivation to be the best graduate student in his group. Mr. B. was briefly screened by the CAPA low fee treatment program, and referred to me for further evaluation and treatment, using Skype. He impressed me by how well he had prepared to undertake the treatment. He had given thought to the times that he and I could arrange treatment sessions, and how he could fit it in between his various classes, supervisions, optional "trainings," and the clinical work required by his program, as well as a part-time job he had at a local psychology clinic.

We began at twice weekly for a few weeks. The patient spoke frankly and with care to report exactly what he was experiencing as his feelings and thoughts occurred to him. He had a sense of humor and often reported his feelings as humorous asides, but he displayed a demanding set of expectations of himself and others. For example, when he experienced angry and negative feelings toward a faculty person or to a disorganized fellow student, he would muse as to whether this represented "splitting" and, if so, did that mean he was a borderline? One time early in the treatment, I expressed an opinion about a minor matter, and he sniffed, "Hmmph! What would Freud say?" We quickly moved to three times a week, face-to-face. The patient's apartment was not set up to use the computer in a room with a couch or a bed. Although he was frank, there was a sense of distance and formality about him, and a preoccupation with himself that made me wonder if the couch would foster greater detachment and remoteness, or whether the difficulty of setting up a couch in a room with computer access was a resistance to greater informality and closeness that he feared.

The patient was extraordinarily ambitious and scrupulous in his writing of case summaries for his job and for supervision, summaries of the readings for each week's classes, and other such work, often working late into the night and through the weekends. He rarely had any fun. His spouse had a similarly busy schedule, and they seemed to have only brief periods of time each week to spend with each other. Occasionally he reported mild bickering between them, but no outright fights, even though I got a sense of the spouse's greater availability and mild disappointment in the patient's lack of availability that the patient himself seemed to miss. So tenaciously dedicated was the patient that I was reminded of a cartoon character called "The Brain" on a television series, "Pinky and the Brain," that my children used to watch. This character was always scheming about how to fulfill his ambition to take over the world. But, there was much that was likable about my patient, despite his stilted and guarded presence, and I could clearly feel that he was suffering. I could hear how admired and respected he was by his contemporaries, even though he could not really appreciate why.

We searched together for ways to understand this ambition. The patient recalled being an average and nonchalant student as a young boy, but he had wanted to go to a prestigious secondary school. When he was admitted, he was shocked to discover how bright the other students were, and so he dedicated himself to studying in order to succeed at something. He believed that his athletic ability was only average, that his looks were the same. His evidence for this was the remarks made in his presence about other students who were considered extremely good-looking and attractive. The patient abandoned sports, consciously adopted plain clothes, and never did anything to call attention to his appearance, lest he had tried at something and failed. He said that his younger brother was considered extremely handsome and his older sister was artistic. He felt inadequate compared to them. Academic success became the venue in which he would gain distinction. It then emerged that he had abandoned his business career because he had come to believe that great success was not attainable, and that he would be, at best, moderately prosperous, but not one of the elite. I wondered to myself what would become of the patient's psychology career, and to the analysis, if he were to experience a similar disillusionment. To date, however, the analytic work has slowly deepened as the patient has become able to experience feelings of sadness in the sessions that he doesn't understand. We are piecing them together as transference wishes displaced onto the parents of his patients, onto faculty members, and supervisors in the CAPA program.

Will it turn out that it will be safer for him to displace these feelings onto his analyst than to experience these disappointments directly with his parents, primarily his mother, disappointments at not being loved or regarded as special in some way that would have provided him with good self-esteem and confidence? Would these feelings emerge more powerfully on the couch or in face-to-face sessions? Will the medium of Skype facilitate or interfere with this process? The answers to these questions remain to be discovered. My preliminary feelings are that the answers are "Skype neutral." I was asked to present a case at a seminar on psychoanalytic assessment, and purposely presented the case without revealing that the patient resided in China and that we were working on Skype. The assembled students and faculty remarked on the analyzability of the patient and the richness of the material. They were astounded when I revealed that the patient lived in China and that we met at a computer-to-computer interface.

I, too, participated in the CAPA China Study Program and visited the city where Mr. B. lived and worked. I told him that we were coming and proposed that we meet face-to-face. While I was excited about the prospect of the meeting, my patient was cautious and a little apprehensive. "Would it interfere with the analysis, and what would we accomplish?" he wondered.

He wasn't sure he had the evening times available, and the mechanics of communicating and setting up the appointment were complicated because of the uncertainties of Internet and telephonic availability. Nevertheless, I arranged a meeting room at my hotel, sent my patient a message, and he showed up right on time for our appointment.

Our meeting was awkward, as we sat at a ninety-degree angle from each other. He barely made eye contact, and we exchanged pleasantries after he said that he didn't feel that we could have a regular session in such unaccustomed circumstances. He remarked that I looked thinner than on Skype, and wondered how he looked different to me. I had already noticed that he had dressed up, gotten a haircut, and taken some care in his appearance. When I mentioned this, he did not respond directly, and seemed uncomfortable. We spent forty-five minutes together discussing the CAPA program, our sightseeing schedule, and some of the events planned for our visit, and parted cordially, but unproductively. When I returned to the United States, and we resumed our scheduled appointments, we fell back into our regular routine. Mr. B. echoed my feelings that the face-to-face meeting had been pleasant but unproductive, and he returned to his regular analytic mode.

It has been recommended by the IPA (Scharff, 2009) that a face-to-face period of analysis and the establishment of an analytic process are essential prior to embarking on a telephonic (or Skype) analysis. Most Skype analyses of mainland Chinese do not offer this possibility at the outset, and my experience with Mr. B. raises the question as to whether this should be a hard and fast rule, and why, in some instances, face-to-face meetings will be disruptive. Akhtar (2010), upon hearing a verbal account of this experience, pointed out the relevance of the waking screen concept (Akhtar, 2009) as described by Pacella (1980) as being involved in this defensive reaction of both the patient and analyst in this instance. Akhtar writes: ". . . the waking screen denotes the background of perceptual experience derived from the earliest exposure to the external world (e.g., its smells, sounds, skin color of significant others, types of trees and houses, etc.). The background of expectations plays "an active role in scanning, integrating, rejecting, or modifying all the new percepts of object representations throughout life" (p.130). Clearly, Akhtar's observation is that the waking screen is, for this analytic pair, the computer screen; it represents the background of perceptual experience for us both. Its absence at the face-to-face encounter required the patient and the analyst to resort to defensive postures that temporarily interrupted the analytic continuum.

ANSWERS TO FREQUENTLY ASKED QUESTIONS ABOUT SKYPE ANALYSES IN CHINA

1. How does analysis of Chinese patients on Skype differ from analysis in the usual setting?

Psychoanalysts listen to the "music" as well as to the words. We pay attention to the rate and rhythm of what is said, to spontaneity or to its interruption, in order to appreciate defenses, resistances, and the state of the transference, and to our own feelings, thoughts, and fantasies, in order to identify and use our countertransference. We tune into the expression of emotion in all of its nuances, to infer wholeheartedness, tentativeness, or even feelings opposite to the words being spoken. Skype neither adds nor detracts from this therapeutic endeavor. But, it does change its familiar characteristics, changes that we must learn to identify and to become familiar with.

Alterations in the analytic process are also brought about by other factors—those of vocabulary, language, education, and the myriad of cultural, and microcultural individualities that have always challenged psychoanalysts in the course of their search for empathy and clarity. Overall, the work goes a little slower. In working with Chinese patients, language and pronunciation can be challenging in some cases, while in others, they create minimal problems for the psychoanalyst. One must be alert for subtle deficits in affective precision and a lack of congruence in the meaning of the words that one hears and in what one says. With the inevitable pauses, one must differentiate the search for the right English word from the need to disguise or distort. The extra care needed to make interventions understandable, may add ponderousness to the interaction, and rob it of emotional immediacy.

Then, too, the quality of connection in a virtual treatment is different than the office setting. First, the portability of the laptop and the worldwide access to the web allows both patient and analyst to continue treatment from a variety of locations, in addition to the office. Any room in the home, any place in the world, a hotel room, even an Internet café, may be used for a session. On the other hand, the analyst, by switching rooms, may stimulate transference fantasies about the analyst living in a mansion. Skype gives each participant a direct look into the other's world.

Such factors result in a change in the quality of connection and attention in the analytic relationship. It is not so much that the use of Skype and these other issues make the analyst's attention better or worse, but rather, they make it different. The analyst must be aware of the tension between "free floating attention" and "attention floating free." The entire world, via the Internet, is available at the analyst's fingertips, and coupled with his or her predilection for multitasking, it may tempt the analyst to engage his mind away from the patient during a heartfelt but, nevertheless, halting and awkwardly expressed statement. A whole new way of identifying one's counter-transference derivatives is now available. Exposed by this new perspective, they become just as evident to the analyst using Skype, with experience and the effort of self-analysis, as to the one sitting behind the patient.

In addition to self-analysis, there are steps that one can take to increase focus and attention. One, for example, is to make the Skype window so large that it occupies the entire screen. This eliminates the distractions of other windows, such as email programs that show newly arriving messages and tempt the analyst to take a peek. There is a decrease in the picture quality when the image fills the entire screen, but this is of less importance than the quality of the analyst's attention.

But, it is not only the issue of attentional rigor that is raised by the use of this new medium. There is also the issue of the "virtual boundary" between the analyst and the patient. This is a boundary that simultaneously exists and doesn't exist. By being aware of it, the analyst can learn much about the countertransference. When the analyst and patient are in the same room, the analyst can reach out and touch the patient, and of course the patient can do the same. With actual touch, it is clear to both parties that a boundary cross-ing has occurred. But, in a virtual medium such as Skype, the analyst or the patient can "reach out and touch" the other's image with his cursor, and the other remains unaware of it. It is a secret boundary crossing, an extension of a thought or fantasy, like many that occur in the face-to-face setting, in which only the fantasy of touching occurs, but hopefully gets recognized, analyzed and used constructively. With Skype, one becomes much more aware of such fantasies, because one experiences this secret action, physically as well as mentally, while the other remains unaware of it. Does the medium intensify such phenomena or does it merely objectify and clarify their existence? Such phenomena, and how to bring them into the analysis, remain to be explored and reported.

2. Is Skype secure?

As has been emphasized throughout this chapter, computer-to-computer communication using Skype software is completely secure and unhackable. Security experts have verified this. Once the connection is broken, there is no record of the communication. The session is as private as any session in one's office. Skype chats and phone conversations, however, are not secure, because they are not encrypted. They are as insecure as all telephone conver-sations. For this reason, they are not used for Skype analyses.

3. Is remote analysis in China politically dangerous for the Chinese patient?

Such an assertion was made in a recent psychoanalytic publication ("Author's name withheld by request," 2008). It wrongfully politicized, fearmongered, and distorted the situation in China (See, also, Letters to the Editor, 2008). The Chinese government cannot eavesdrop on a Skype computer-to-computer analytic session. Moreover, CAPA patients are mental health professionals, who are invested in a self-exploration in an effort to become better clinicians. They are not concerned about political consequences for themselves or their patients. They have been asked about this on numerous occasions, and speak frankly during their analytic sessions, except for the usual defensive interferences with free association. The likelihood of political dissidents becoming CAPA patients or patients of CAPA students is negligible. The reality is that the Chinese government has been very supportive of CAPA psychodynamic training programs, because of the small number of well-trained clinicians throughout China. CAPA provides a much-needed service in China.

4. What if the patient has a crisis or become suicidal?

CAPA has experienced Chinese psychiatrists in each city where it offers Skype treatment. They would act as liaisons in the event of an emergency. To date, such a situation has not occurred.

5. Does the analysis of inhibitions in a person living in a repressive political regime predispose him to personal danger?

This is a complicated issue that, at first glance, may seem to have an obvious answer: of course, a patient, freed of constraint by analysis of inhibition, will find the lack of free choice less tolerable, and hence will be more vulnerable in a repressive society. A colleague involved in CAPA analysis related the following incident. Her patient was transferred from her position in a psychiatric hospital because she spoke out against certain hospital policies, which she found oppressive. But, perhaps the issue is framed simplistically. The patient may have acted out certain oppositional impulses that are a part of her character structure. Farther along in her analysis, they might well be handled in a more mature, less self-destructive manner. This incident is really not so different from what might take place anywhere, given a hierarchically structured work environment. Such situations are quite common in all societies, regardless of the political system. Analysts in any setting have had patients who suffer from the consequences of such actions, and analysts everywhere worry that the analytic work itself may have resulted in actions that harmed their patients, but analysts do not routinely encourage their patients to action. Patients living in repressive societies often have an acute sense of the danger involved in speaking out and can distinguish between the danger from outside and the danger within. China may be less repressive than most Americans think. People speak freely, loudly and in public places about their objections to government policies. Apparently, what the government is concerned about is public protest in the streets and public media.

6. Is malpractice insurance available or necessary for treating Chinese patients?

Since psychoanalysis is not a recognized or licensed profession in China, no liability insurance is required. A Chinese patient would have to travel to the United States to initiate a lawsuit against an analyst. Obviously, the probability of such an occurrence is very low. Private practitioners in China do not have malpractice insurance and, indeed, it may not be available.

7. How does the Skype experience compare to telephone analysis?

There is no comparison. The opportunity to see the patient, in addition to hearing the narrative, adds to the subtlety and completeness of communication, and approaches the condition of the analytic pair meeting in the same room. The patient is as close as the analyst's computer screen.

CONCLUDING REMARKS

We have attempted to convey the history, the technical aspects, and the gratifications as well as the difficulties of conducting Skype analyses with Chinese patients. We have also discussed the similarities and differences between Skype analysis and analysis done in the office, and have presented two case histories of analytic treatment using Skype to illustrate our points. We have answered several frequently asked questions about this work. The modality of distance analysis is in its infancy, but it may well be the wave of the future, with respect to providing treatment to any patient, including patients close enough to come to the office. A recent article in *Psychiatric News* (Daly, 2010) reports that states are increasingly requiring malpractice carriers to cover telemedicine. This development will provide greater accessibility for patients who, for a variety of reasons, might be unable to be physically present in the office.

Chapter Nine

Separation, Sex, Superego, and Skype[1]

Jerome S. Blackman

At the 1964 World's Fair in New York City, the AT&T Pavilion featured an exhibit I remember fairly well. It consisted of two rooms or booths, each with a telephone that had a black and white TV screen on it. On the screen, as you were speaking to the other room's occupants, you could see the callers on your screen, and they could see and talk to you on theirs. My high school buddies (and I, I hesitate to confess) broke into two groups, one in each room, and after a few minutes proceeded to make obscene gestures at each other over the "Picturephone."[2] As I reflect back on that incident, I think our clowning around was at least partially facilitated by the presence of the electronic interface.

Now, forty-six years later, videophones have become popular in Japan (video cellphones). In early 2010, Schmohl (2010) predicted that they would appear soon in other countries. Following his prediction, Apple released the iPhone 4 in June 2010, which includes a live video feed of the person on the other end. In the United States, stationary Picturephones appeared briefly in the 1980s and 1990s, but were so large, immobile, and expensive that they never caught on. Is it a coincidence, or has there been a persistent resistance to using these devices in the United States caused by a nationally based inhibition acting as a defense against shame over our sexual and aggressive drive-related antics at the 1964 World's Fair?[3]

Fast-forward to the 1990s. First there was instant messaging. Then today's "texting" developed—mostly among teenagers. They, not terribly dissimilarly from their forebears almost fifty years ago, eventually (and no doubt predictably) turned texting into "sexting." Sexting involves sending ribald messages (and sometimes nude photos) to other teens using the various Internet and phone conduits now available. A fascinating look at the potential "nth degree" of sexting is to be found in a rather salacious murder mystery by Sandra Brown (2003). In her book, *Hello Darkness*, a male pedophile infiltrates a teen hookup location that had been set up by two spoiled, sexually predatory adolescent girls. He finds victims by monitoring the kids' interactive website—which is called, appropriately, the "Sex Club." Perhaps not surprisingly, sexting and scandalous Facebook pages are hidden from parents—the curious marriage of autonomy and sexuality that has characterized American adolescent individuation since . . . well, at least since eighteen-year-old Josie Marcus ran away from her middle-class Jewish parents in San Francisco, wound up living with a crooked sheriff in Tombstone, and eventually left him to "marry" the gambler-turned-gunman-turned-lawman-turned-entrepreneur, the ultimate bad boy, Wyatt Earp. [4]

Besides the possible sexual and separation symbolism of mobile phones and high speed Internet access, both have reality significance. Practically speaking, most teenagers seem to "need" a cell phone, not just as a sign of individuation from parents (often necessary for making friends) but as an entry to social fora. My twenty-one-year-old son has observed that teens and young adults *need both* Internet and in-person social skills. In his view, Facebook, Twitter, texting, and email each require different forms of "etiquette," and young businesspeople need abilities in each of these venues for networking and career advancement. He has opined that avoidance of Internet communications for his generation would be analogous to avoidance of telephone communications for my generation. [5] An example of how the Internet boon to adolescent individuation and socialization can go awry is the case of Lori Drew. She and her daughter created a fictitious teenage boy named Josh Evans who, through MySpace, first flirted with and then rejected Megan Meier. Megan then killed herself, and the case wound up in criminal court. (Hufstutter, 2007).

The above facets of electronic communications suggest certain tentative conclusions: 1) they have practical social and business uses; 2) they can become part of a plethora of symbolic human interactions; 3) they can be used for nefarious purposes. Following on these preliminary formulations, but perhaps at the risk of being accused of splitting, I believe that when it comes to programs like Skype, there is good news and there is bad news. [6]

THE GOOD NEWS

The good news is that free, software-based video-conferencing enhances and possibly helps "secure"[7] a large variety of warm, close relationships. For example, Dr. N, on starting his final year of psychiatry residency, was upset when his wife accepted (matched with) a position in a residency program in her medical specialty that was over five hundred miles away. She accepted it and, of necessity, took with her their two-and-a-half-year-old son, who was also very attached to his father. The solution to their one-year separation was Skype, which allowed Dr. N to see and talk to his son every day. This reduced his son's "father hunger" (Herzog, 1980, 2004), fostered the final elements of his son's individuation, and prevented pathological oedipal victory dynamics in the boy. The father also flew to visit when he could get away on weekends during that year. When Dr. N finished his residency, he found work where his wife was taking her residency. The father and son continue to enjoy a strong bond now, years later.

Further, videoconferencing and e-matching for dating can also, to a certain extent, replace blind dates. This can save time and aggravation and provide more safety than, for example, meeting people in bars. A couple I know met through an e-dating service and Skyped before meeting in person. He is a researcher at a medical school, and she is an attorney who spent long hours, for years, working to make partner at her firm. Both had had little time to attend social outings and events. They most likely would never have met save through e-dating.

In addition, videoconferencing allows parents to contact *gratis* their children who live large distances away and/or are attending college. A peculiarity of many current-day U.S. university dormitories, which routinely provide no "land-line" telephones, is that they have terrible cell phone reception but excellent Wi-Fi. Computers (with Skype, for example) therefore offer more reliable (secure-organized?) connections than cellphones. A sixty-six-year-old woman friend mentioned at a party on one Saturday evening that she had spent the afternoon (eastern time) Skyping her son and grandchildren (who live on the West Coast). Their visit would have been impossible but for videoconferencing.

Video-conferenced Treatment and Teaching

Comments in Regard to Dr. Lana Fishkin's Skype Analysis of a Patient in China

Continuing for a moment on this theme of positive relationships, Drs. Ralph and Lana Fishkin deftly describe how videoconferencing has made analytic psychotherapies available in China. Dr. L. Fishkin found little difference in establishing trust, interpreting transference and defense, and thereby relieving difficulties in a normal-neurotic young woman who had experienced unresolved object loss. The 7,000-mile divide (between Philadelphia and China) had almost no effect on the establishment and maintenance of a clear object image of the analyst. The analyst used the usual interpretive techniques to treat her patient's conflict-based inhibition of aggression, which apparently was defending against guilt and fear of loss of the object. A stable treatment alliance was achieved quickly and persevered. Dr. L. Fishkin's subsequent in-person meeting with her patient, in China, was experienced as pleasant and engaging for both analyst and analysand, and the analysand remarked that it felt very much the same as the videoconferenced sessions. My impression is that self and object constancy had not been a particular problem for the patient, and therefore did not need to be handled during treatment.

Another point of interest in Dr. L. Fishkin's report of the treatment is that sexual material was not forthcoming. Dr. L. Fishkin's formulation that this omission might be cultural brings up an issue that often occurs during analytic therapies. I agree with her that certain superego identifications are more prevalent in certain groups of people, producing cultural values. One Chinese woman also told me that sweetness (inhibition of aggression) was a culturally preferred value for Chinese girls. An interesting theoretical problem concerns how much to value identifications with sources other than parents (for example, media, peers, TV, teachers, members of the opposite sex). These need to be contrasted with people's identifications with parents—identifications with the lost object and with the aggressor (Sandler, 1960)—which later may be externalized onto some group, intellectualized, generalized, and normalized. For example, sweetness was also emphasized in a forty-year-old American male patient's childhood. He was raised in the South, and was supposed to be a "gentleman," although both of his parents were serious alcoholics. His mother forced him to attend "cotillion," a dressy, antebellum-style dance with specially selected other children, when he was in grade school. He simultaneously hated cotillion but "obeyed" his mother. Although he blamed the cotillion for creating his conflicts about activity/passivity, respect/disobedience, and sexual inhibitions, that was only a small part of the story. More powerful compromise formations involved his intrasystemic ego conflict—namely identification with his mother vs. disidentification from her. He also experienced an intersystemic conflict between hostile-aggression (used for autonomy) and guilt, resulting in the defenses of reaction-formations, passivity, and mild alcoholism.

In other words, there seem to be symmetric pitfalls in assessing culture. We may focus on the effects of "culture" and thereby undervalue identifications and intrapsychic conflict; or we may view complaints of culture too intrapsychically and underestimate the powerful effects of the cultural milieu in which the child develops.[8] The more that Internet communications with peers are out of the control of parents, the more the effects of that "surround" (Spitz and Cobliner, 1966) are likely to hold sway, and identifications with parents be diminished in effect. We certainly see this phenomenon in adolescents, in any culture, who join gangs when their parents are neglectful or disinterested.

Considering the possible cultural inhibitions of expression of sexual drive verbalizations in China, or perhaps due to those urges, when I was invited to lecture, both in Shanghai and in Beijing (in person), the most requested talk was "Why Men Have Extramarital Affairs." In this lecture, I described the ten character types suggested by Marcus (2004); I also mentioned interpersonal stresses, developmental delays, neurotic inhibitions, obsessions, conversions, psychopathy, and psychoses as differential diagnoses. During the question and answer period, I was told of other variations in dynamics causing Chinese men to philander. One is the male bureaucrat who hands out favors to women who trade sexual activity for them (narcissistic power dynamics). Again, although the Chinese professionals who mentioned this type thought of it as a Chinese phenomenon, that sort of misbehavior has no doubt existed from time immemorial in any political structure where a narcissistic and/or psychopathic male has achieved a position of power. Another interesting, perhaps more common male character in China is governed by severe shame. A student in China presented, during a video class, a case vignette of a married man who, after admitting to his wife that he had had a one-night stand with another woman, was insisting on getting a divorce. His wife, the patient, did not want this, and was willing to forgive him and try to work things out. Although he apparently was not involved emotionally with the other woman, he felt he had brought such shame on the family (loss of face), that he did not deserve his wife's forgiveness.[9]

Finally, concerning the issue of inhibitions regarding expression of sexuality in Chinese women, one must consider that this is not entirely culture-dependent. Even in the United States in 2010, at the height of our culture's "openness," adult women generally still experience much more defensive activity guarding against shame (especially about masturbation) than men. Below, I discuss some of the vicissitudes of the availability of Internet porn for men. When it comes to entertaining sexual fantasies, many adult women still prefer so-called "chick flicks"[10] and "chick-lit," both of which center around love, romance, betrayal, and troubles, typically, with a male sexual partner's attentiveness to the woman and her feelings.[11] Impersonal, X-rated sexuality is generally not appealing to adult women (Marcus, 1980), although supposedly increasing among adolescent girls and young adult women.[12] Nevertheless, a Google search for "most popular online games for girls" turned up, among some others, "dressupkiss.com." This website features "love games, kissing games, makeup games, and naughty games."[13] In my lengthy time in psychiatry, I have only treated one woman who masturbated while watching graphically pornographic movies at home, alone, whereas this is often a commonplace experience for men at some point in their lives. The multiple developmental reasons for women's relative avoidance of masturbation are noted by Kleeman (1976) and further elaborated by Halber-stadt-Freud (1998).

Comments in Regard to Dr. Ralph Fishkin's Skype Analytic Psychotherapy of a Patient in China

Turning to a patient with different psychic structure, Dr. Ralph Fishkin explicated his fascinating findings from Skype treatment of an apparently ambitious, compulsive Chinese man who gave up working in business in order to study psychology. The patient and his wife had decided to have no children, apparently for practical reasons relating to their careers. Although open during Skype sessions, the patient had difficulty relating in person when he and Dr. R. Fishkin met in China some time after the therapy had been in progress. For this patient, the 7,000 miles had evidently represented what Akhtar (1992) has called "optimal distance." The distance in that case, apparently, had defensively relieved self-object fusion and/or identity diffusion anxiety. At Dr. R. Fishkin's "live" meeting with his patient in China, the patient avoided eye contact and became guarded. What appears to have occurred is that the patient's object relations difficulties became more acutely observable in person, due to the increased emotional closeness. In this case, the use of Skype seemed to make the treatment more workable since it allowed more emotional distance, at least in the short run.

Parenthetically, this case also raises an interesting theoretical question about couples who decide not to have children. Although as Westerners we believe it is a major step forward that women no longer feel they must bear children, and China, at the time of this writing, has a one-child policy, these social elements may complicate our formulations about people we treat. I have found that many of the people I have evaluated, both male and female, who have no interest in having children, suffer with deficits in their capacities for warmth, empathy, trust, closeness, and stability, and many have limited affect tolerance associated with those object relations problems.

One married woman, Ms. X, who had persuaded her husband not to have children, consulted me for anxiety. This symptom had erupted when the man with whom she had been having a decades-long sexual affair suddenly decided he wanted to leave his wife and marry Ms. X, which would have required her to leave her husband (who had never guessed at the affair). Her "two-man phenomenon" (Goldberger, 1988) guarded her against both self-object fusion anxiety (too much closeness with one man) and separation anxiety (being alone when not with each man). Patients like Ms. X have sometimes reached a well-reasoned conclusion that they would be inadequate and/or unhappy parents, at least unless they avail themselves of long-term intensive psychotherapy.

One must consider differential diagnosis, however: not everyone who avoids having children has object relations problems. For example, Renee (Blackman, 2001) had initially agreed to a "no child" agreement when she married her older husband who already had had children with his first wife.

After several years of marriage, however, she developed a wish for a child associated with love for her husband. Her conflict about this caused her to consult me. During her brief dynamic psychotherapy, we clarified that she had originally defensively inhibited a wish for children to guard against a guilty feeling that she would be a bad mother. But her fear that she would be a "bad" mother turned out to be a fantasy based on an unconscious identification with her own mother, who had been overwhelmed by raising five children. Renee had also guarded against shame over possibly becoming "too dependant" on her husband during pregnancy and afterward. The no-child solution to this conflict had guarded her from anxiety emanating from a father-transference to her husband, who she feared would become tyrannical (like her father) if she depended on him too much. Once she understood these dynamics, she discussed the matter with her husband, who, it turned out, had been harboring wishes to have children with her, but had been reticent about it. At that point, we ended treatment, and over the next three years, the patient sent me photos of her two new children, along with notes of pleasure and thanks. Her original no-child decision had not been based on culture, practicality, nor object relations deficits. Rather, unconscious conflict had led her to make an ego-syntonic decision, at the time of her marriage, which turned out to be a maladaptive compromise formation some years later.

Videoteaching

Further good news about Internet communications. My own experience in videoteaching analytic theory to Chinese professionals and in supervising psychoanalytic psychotherapy cases in Shanghai and Beijing (through CAPA[14]) has been exhilarating. The students integrate the knowledge base and relate it to themselves, their patients, and their culture. In a recent class on technique based on defense theory, I was pointing out how, in adults, dedifferentiation (Mahler, 1968; Blackman, 2003) could defend against shame and loss of the object's love. Several students became interested in this defensive operation as it might pertain to Chinese families' traditional value of children's "obedience." A discussion ensued of the effects on superego development of the sense of identity when dedifferentiation and passivity are encouraged in children.[15]

Another surprisingly pleasurable Skype discussion with my Chinese students evolved in response to my suggestions for using inductive reasoning as one method for detecting patients' unconscious defenses (Blackman, 2003). I mentioned that a patient is likely using defenses if you, the therapist, experience a break in empathy with the patient or think the person you are treating is giving you a lot of "bull." My clumsy efforts to explain this slang idiom by eventually describing it as "the feces of the husband of the cow," led to general hilarity in the class and confirmation that the same concept exists in the Chinese language! (The phrase the students taught me involves dogs.) I also walked away from that class more convinced than ever of the universal invasion of language by drive elements (in this case, mostly anal), even when the language components are pictographs and people are convening from 7,000 miles away with a twelve-hour time difference. Moreover, it suggested how sharing of (especially preoedipal) drive derivatives on the Internet can sometimes advance social connectedness and learning, much as that activity may do so in face-to-face friendships.[16]

THE BAD NEWS

Now for the bad news. Drive breakthrough seems to be a bit more of a liability for either side of the Skype interface—probably because the physical separation reduces anxiety and causes a slight diminution in resonance-empathy (Buie, 1981).[17] Other types of empathy are less diminished (such as having had the same experience, using creative imagination, or understanding through dynamic formulation). In teaching with Skype, I have heard more personal material, on average, than in in-person classes. This has not been necessarily negative, but required understanding that the usual repressive mechanisms could be diluted by the Internet.

For example, a female therapist in China, Dr. Chang, presented a case vignette about Mu Ling, a twenty-seven-year-old single woman, to me during a video-conferenced class on countertransference. Mu Ling's chief complaint was a moderate social phobia complicated by a tendency to reject men who fell in love with her. Dr. Chang soon learned that Mu Ling was consciously trying to suppress a shameful urge to look at men's crotches. After the therapist had presented this case at another case conference, she, herself, had felt guilty about making the presentation without Mu Ling's explicit permission. The therapist wondered if her own embarrassment and guilt constituted a countertransference of some kind. I opined that it sounded like a concordant identification (Racker, 1953); i.e., Dr. Chang had possibly, at least in part, identified with Mu Ling's conflicts about exposure.

Based on the almost ubiquitous use of projection (as well as symbolization) in phobias, I offered a conjecture that, aside from Mu Ling consciously wishing to look at a man's genitals, she unconsciously wished to expose her own genitals to a man. Both her voyeuristic and exhibitionistic wishes no doubt conflicted with shame, leading Mu Ling to become anxious in public (agoraphobia)—due to projection of the wishes and to externalization of her superego—and inhibited with men she dated. I said that I thought Dr. Chang had transiently identified with these conflicts, and then felt ashamed (and guilty) about making any further exposure of Mu Ling in a case conference.

Some days after class, Dr. Chang sent me an email detailing elements of the case and further confirming her own countertransference. It is with Dr. Chang's explicit written permission that I reproduce some of her email here:[18]

Dear Jerry,

Many thanks for your interpret and encourage me send you this case. That made me refreshed suddenly. In the class, I have no time to tell you the most interesting thing about my case and myself. Let me expose it first:

In this session, I felt more relax and close to Mu Ling. At the night, before sleep, I think about Mu Ling again. She's afraid of expose herself what? I also have same feeling before several years ago, till now I still have it sometimes. Taking this question, I fall in sleep, then got a dream in Saturday morning. Seems there is an answer in it: "I lie on the bed, catch sight of my penis. It's fresh and strong, smooth and long, straight up like a pen, as thin as finger. I don't feel surprise. I know I have it, too!

"I want to hide it, feel shy, and I won't want others see it."

"I look at him, a middle-age man, lie on opposite side of the bed, his penis is thick and relaxed. He is still sleeping. Seems there is a middle age woman sleeping beside him. I can't see her clearly."

I think this dream is telling my Oedipus complex. I yearn for father's penis, identify with father, hope myself was a boy, have more power, energy and success. I deny my female identity, so I can't see mother clearly, hope she was invisible. Penis like a pen, that means I want to have more achievement on writing . . . Presenting a case like this in English is my first time. It's very hard but very useful. Striving for my patient . . . also make me feel stronger. I'm eager for showing myself, but also afraid of that, want to hide it, my ambition and competitive power, like before.

Today (after Jerry's class) I remembered a film, Princess Diary. I have seen it thousand times. That's a Cinderella story, an invisible, inferior teenager finally become a bright, responsible, brave princess. That's also my dream.

Further regarding this case, Dr. Chang wrote about a session where they were discussing a sexual relationship Mu Ling had had with a boy in high school. Mu Ling worried, "Am I really too free in my behavior?" further indicating her intrapsychic conflicts between sexual wishes and superego. Mu Ling later clarified that she looked at men using her "peripheral vision," a phenomenon she had looked up on the Internet(!). Dr. Chang reported: Mu Ling said, "I keep thinking about . . . peripheral vision. Just sometimes, it's [like] . . . the mind divide into 2 parts: one is think [about] the matter [about which] he is talking, the other [has an] . . . unconscious worry . . . This [is a] kind of cock-bottom thought that will be discovered." (It should be "rock-bottom," a very interesting clerical error. Cock also means penis.) Later, Mu Ling said, regarding a particular man, ". . . I dreamed that he felt I was a bad person, had bad character," i.e. Mu Ling continued to demonstrate her conflicts among sexuality, aggression, and guilt, as well as the resultant externalization.

Autistic Defense, Regression, and Avatars

Regarding the topics of intrapsychic and object relations conflicts, the April 2010 Margaret Mahler Symposium in Philadelphia, which included many of the papers in this book, was replete with examples of children and adolescents using the Internet as a sort of autistic defense. Presenters reported on teenagers who would lose themselves in chat rooms. Some split their identities, experiencing self-disintegration and sometimes transient psychotic episodes. Others, on Facebook, MySpace, and other venues, created false identities representative of difficulties with inauthenticity. The Internet certainly encourages autistic withdrawal into fantasy, but there is real money to be made! *Second Life* is an extraordinarily popular website, started several years ago, where you choose your own avatar. You can interact with the avatars of others, take courses at avatar universities, and, in general, involve yourself in art imitating life. More recently, businesses such as Warner Brothers, Northrop-Grumman, and IBM (Morrison, 2009) have established living and non-living avatars (buildings) in *Second Life,* and some retailers are literally selling virtual real estate and trinkets for *real* dollars. There is even news of medical schools and mental health training centers turning to *Second Life* (*Big Pond News*, 2010). The danger of vulnerable teenagers (and adults) getting caught in the web of Second Life and such websites, and even squandering money, cannot be minimized.

In my practice, I have evaluated teenagers after they got in trouble (with some authority, usually a school) for making violent threats toward others on the Internet. When seen ("in person") in my office, they were regularly ashamed and contrite. It seemed the Internet had caused a temporary dilution of—or regression in—superego functioning and impulse control. This same phenomenon, comprising autistic defense, impulse discharge, and superego regression involving sexual elements, is also common in adults using the Internet in chat rooms or email. The caseload of many employment lawyers is filled with examples of accusations of sexual harassment over the Internet.

Internet Porn

When addressing sex and the Internet, we are led, as day leads to night, to the complex topic of Internet pornography. A recent article in the *Wall Street Journal* documented that the United States Security and Exchange Commission's Inspector General found thirty-three employees or contractors had violated SEC rules by viewing Internet porn during working hours. Although the thirty-three represented less than 1 percent of SEC's employees, ". . . 17

were senior officials whose salaries ranged from $100,000 to $222,000" per year. "A senior attorney at SEC's headquarters . . . spent eight hours [per workday] accessing Internet porn" (Orol, April 23, 2010).

In addition to that negative effect of Internet porn (i.e., ego regression in work capacity due to the availability of sexual material), there is much more to be said about this topic. I will briefly try to cover some of the more salient issues. To begin with, there is the problem of addiction to porn. A Google search (in May 2010) of the term "porn addiction" drew 1,570,000 hits. According to one source, there are 372 million web pages on 4.3 million pornographic websites; 72 million people visit porn sites per year; the largest consumer of Internet porn is the twelve- to seventeen-year-old age group; and 10 percent of adults supposedly admit to Internet porn addiction (Brigham Young University, 2010). According to another website, $97 billion was earned worldwide on porn in 2006, $2.84 billion of it generated on the Internet. According to this site, 96 percent of visitors to porn sites were male, 4 percent female (Family Safe Media, 2006). These statistics, though no doubt contestable, still afford a ballpark idea of the magnitude of this issue, predominantly among males, throughout the world.

Authors such as Andrea Dworkin (1981) repeatedly pointed out that porn is degrading to women and that most of it tends to portray women inhumanly and unrealistically.[19] One result of such portrayal may be, in vulnerable boys, the development of impossible expectations of normal girls, and later, of normal women. Person's (1986) studies of men's conscious sexual fantasies were quite revealing: the most common erotic fantasy in men was the "omni-available woman . . . for men the woman's availability, ready sexuality, and unqualified approval constitute a major common thread. It is her availability and enthusiasm that bolster his virility" (p. 8). Inflammation of that expectation is counter to empathic ties between men and women, and is thereby counterproductive if mutual empathy is desired by couples in adulthood.

An even more disturbing problem is child pornography. Although this reprehensible activity is illegal in the United States and many other countries, it is still flourishing on the Internet. In addition, the availability of digital and cellphone cameras and the ease of posting of photos on the Internet set the stage for humiliating, impulsive acts by middle- and high-school pranksters.

Notwithstanding these persuasive arguments, censorship can lead to deplorable situations such as the one in China in January 2010, when the Ministry of Public Security arrested 5,394 people for simply downloading and watching porn (Buckley, 2010).

Porn in Adolescence

To add fuel to the fire, it has been argued that easily obtainable masturbatory material, especially for teenage boys, could protect society (BBC News,

2002) and/or enhance the boys' psychological development. Meers (1975) found that early teenage boys who experience shame over masturbatory urges tended to defensively involve themselves (with girls, who were willing for different reasons) in sexual intercourse at puberty. These same boys rejected any oral elements of sex, as well, and therefore avoided kissing and "petting."

As Meers (1975) and Marcus and Francis (1975) emphasize, masturbation can be good for teenagers as long as it does not become an "addiction" or a compulsion, often to relieve tension. Masturbation gives teenagers relief of sexual tension without embroiling them in a sexual relationship. They thereby avoid emotional turmoil and disturbances in affect regulation (and sometimes in reality testing)—common complications of injecting actual sexual intercourse into highly fantasized and usually symbiotic-style romantic ties with other adolescents (Blos, 1960).

When sexual intercourse is involved in adolescent relationships, fantasies can become reified; later, there will be increased risk of a suicide attempt when the relationship inevitably breaks down. The dynamics of such suicide attempts follow Kohut's (1971) reasoning about dissolution of the self. In adolescence, sexual relationships typically involve fusion of the self-image with the loved object's representation. When the relationship breaks up, there is therefore a breakdown in the self-representation causing release of "aggressive breakdown products." The destructive aggression is frequently turned on the self as a defense against guilt. Because of teens' limited impulse control and affect tolerance, the turning of rage on the self can lead to a suicide attempt. It may be, therefore, that Internet fantasies are safer, as long as they are not terribly overstimulating and do not promote acting out (Rexford, 1966; Paniagua, 1998; Akhtar, 2009).

Interestingly, Internet porn has some other advantageous qualities for adolescent boys that abet them in avoiding the usual objections of parents. First, there are no dirty magazines lying around the house to be picked up and seen by younger siblings—who might suffer the unpleasant negative consequences of sexual overstimulation. In addition, the teenage boy's use of Internet porn can be hidden from his mother and father, thereby 1) avoiding primal scene reversals (Arlow, 1980) where parents are forced to witness their son's sexuality, and 2) utilizing sexuality in the service of adolescent individuation: the porn can be kept unknown from his parents. Also, as is often quipped, no one gets pregnant or an STD from masturbation.

Finally, when adolescents use the Internet for sexual purposes, they avoid breaking the incest barrier. During child development, the first notions of the incest barrier develop, under expeditious circumstances, sometime after the emergence of more or less integrated self and object constancy. The incest barrier further evolves in relation to the vicissitudes of oedipal struggles during the first genital stage; self and object differentiation should thereby be strengthened. During adolescence, it is important that the incest barrier remain intact. Finding sexual stimulation outside the household is part of that developmental task.

Porn and Latency

Under favorable conditions, the incest barrier becomes stronger between the ages of six and eleven, when the typical defenses of reaction-formation, repression, identification, isolation of affect, intellectualization, displacement, sublimation, and denial are so active against sexual thoughts. Knight (2005) found an increase in affect regulation as well. Notwithstanding arguments about the possible benefits during adolescence, Internet porn (and sexual material in the media) is overstimulating to latency children: it disrupts the development of affect regulation, sleep, intellect, concentration, and other ego functions. The overstimulated latency child is more vulnerable to autistic defense, breakthrough of primary process, drive inflammation, and attentional deficits. Also, when children are overstimulated during latency, they are more prone to misbehave postpubertally. When overstimulated latency children reach adolescence proper, with its upsurge of sexual (and aggressive) drive wishes, their predictable exposure to gruesome destructive images and to sexually titillating material (both easily accessed through the click of a mouse) is more likely to provoke attentional deficits and tendencies to act out (and to act up).

Aggression and the Internet

We should not just focus on the problem of problematic sexual elements associated with Internet surfing and communication. Hostile-destructive aggression also rears its (for the most part) ugly head. The most commonly played, Internet-based, real-time game is *World of Warcraft*. It supposedly accounts for 62 percent of the MMORPG[20] games, has annual revenues of over $800 million and boasts over 11.5 million players worldwide. 80 percent of players are male, 48 percent Asian, 22 percent North American, and 17 percent European (*World of Warcraft* Statistics in 2010). This game may act as a sublimation, perhaps draining off animosities (hostile-destructive aggressive wishes [Parens et al., 1994]) that might otherwise lead to real wars or destructive behavior. On the other hand, perhaps the game can be overstimulating and addicting, thus increasing the risk of future inflamed destructive aggression, violent misbehavior, and perhaps a tendency toward more actual wars. One statistic indicates that the average male player in the United States spends 22.7 hours per week playing the game. The implications and effects are, I believe, far from clear, but even so, worrisome.

According to a *New York Times* article in 2007, South Korea had established 140 rehabilitation centers (JUIRS—Jump Up Internet Rescue Schools) to treat Internet addiction. An estimated 30 percent of people under eighteen years of age, in South Korea were addicted to the Internet—chatting and/or playing games more than two hours per day (Fackler, 2007). Many, apparently, were playing *World of Warcraft.* The other South Koreans may be playing *Starcraft,* another real-time game of war that takes place on another planet . The pervasiveness of *Starcraft* in South Korea is astounding: *Starcraft* has its own television channel, and the finalists are virtual rock stars whose final game is presented with hype reminiscent of *American Idol.*[21]

SOME PARTING THOUGHTS

A final word about treatability of adults with interpretive techniques on the Internet. Dynamic therapy, whether in person or over the Internet, requires the person in treatment to possess a quantum of abstraction, integrative functioning, and reality testing; reasonable affect tolerance; a modicum of trust; and a reasonably active superego—especially honesty and reliability (Blackman, 2010). Even if patients are thereby judged to be treatable with interpretive therapy, Dr. L. Fishkin's note about inhibition of sexual material in her patient may be an indication that sensitive, highly conflictual matters may be somewhat less easily accessible by Skype. On the other hand, Dr. R. Fishkin noted more openness (and drive discharge) when using videoconferencing for treatment. My own experience doing Skype-based therapy in China, along with much of the other data I have cited herein above, also suggests a mixed picture. Under certain circumstances, electronic communications seem to foster discharge of sexual and aggressive drive fantasy. Under others, inhibition can become magnified. Possibly analogous to people using the couch, the barrier of the computer screen raises, as well, the potential for ego and superego regression, sudden appearance of basic mistrust, self-object fusion and separation anxieties, affect storms, and the emergence of a considerable variety of defense constellations to manage it all.

NOTES

1. The author would like to thank Janet Schiff, LCSW, FIPA, Susan Stones, LCSW, FIPA, and Theodore and Susan Blackman for their extremely helpful comments and suggestions about this paper.

2. Through the wonders of the Internet, I was able to find confirmation of my memory with more specifics. (Hand, accessed 2010).

3. Ironically, my joke here may contain a grain of truth: one url notes that ". . . AT and T researchers . . . discovered that people did not like using the Picturephone . . . [P]eople did not like the idea of having others see them." (Earth Station, 2010).

4. Josephine Earp (2010). In 1879, Josie had initially run away with her friend, Dora Hirsh, to be an actress and singer. Josie wound up in Tombstone, AZ, where she lived with Johnny Behan, eventually became close to his son from his prior marriage, and apparently stayed close to the son throughout her life. She left Behan for Earp around 1881, and appears to have been the "common-law" wife of Earp until his death forty-six years later. See also Tefertiller (1997), Wyatt Earp (2010), and Lake (1994).

5. Coincidentally, my grandmother, who was born in the 1890s, always disliked talking on the telephone. She never completely adapted to it—she preferred visiting and chatting in person.

6. Just as with electronic communications, good news/bad news setups need not involve splitting—this sort of distinction may involve reality, sexual and/or superego conflicts. A male patient of mine communicated (in person) the following joke: Moses came down from Mt. Sinai with the Ten Commandments. His buddies gathered around and asked, "Mo, how'd you make out?" Moses answered, "Well there's good news and bad news. The good news is I got him down to ten. The bad news is that adultery's still in it."

7. In Ainsworth's sense (Bretherton, 1992).

8. This is one of Erikson's points in *Childhood and Society* (1950). Discussion of these matters was started by Freud (1930). Salient additions were later added by Loewenstein (1951). More recently, Paniagua (2004) has reviewed the interface of culture and intrapsychic structure in Spain, and Akhtar (2005, 2006) has addressed the same factors in India.

9. In this case, since the husband even refused to attend a conjoint session (due to shame), and the wife desperately wanted to save the marriage, I advised the psychotherapy student to encourage the wife to argue with her husband. I suggested the argument should be based on object relatedness—that is, he should consider her feelings about the matter before just punishing himself. He needed to feel guilty about the amount of harm he would bring his family and the emotional pain he would cause them all by deserting them; perhaps these factors would outweigh his wish to relieve his family of shame. (i.e., from a theoretical standpoint, she could attempt to create an intrasystemic conflict in his superego, leading possibly to a different compromise formation as the outcome.) I have to admit that I had never heard of such a case in the United States in over thirty-five years of practice.

10. One of my favorites is *In Her Shoes* (2005).

11. For a serious example of this genre, see Bertrice Small's historical romance novel, *Rosamund* and its compelling sequel, *Until You;* for a more tongue-in-cheek view of the topic, try *Porn for Women* (Cambridge Women's Pornography Cooperative, 2007), which has a picture on the front cover of a barefoot man, dressed in jeans and a work-shirt, who is intently vacuuming a hardwood floor.

12. Hollywood seems to delight in portraying normal women as "on the prowl" for impersonal sex. In the recent movie *Knocked Up*, for example, the female protagonist goes out with friends who encourage her to find a man for a one-night stand to celebrate a job promotion. After acting this out, she finds herself pregnant. She then attempts to develop a relationship with the man she had slept with. (*Knocked Up*, 2007).

13. One example of a "naughty game" involves trying to photograph "Vanessa," an animated young female (and not her bodyguard) in a "compromising" position. Vanessa is gamboling around a pool in a bikini. The "naughtiness" all seems to surround exhibitionism and narcissism, without any graphic sexuality.

14. China American Psychoanalytic Alliance, www.capachina.org

15. There seems to be intrasystemic conflict in many modern Chinese families' superego structure. There is conflict among obedience, independence, caring/sociableness, and excellence/ambition. See Fong (2007). This is most certainly a topic that should be studied analytically in the future.

16. In 2009, I was an invited lecturer at Peking University Department of Psychology and at Shanghai Mental Health Center. I had previously taught the Shanghai group through videoconferencing. Our meetings were a grand reunion of sorts, getting to know each other "for real." In addition, we spent a considerable amount of time eating together (sharing of oral drive elements). During these very engaging interactions, I found the students, who were mostly psychiatrists and psychologists, to be somewhat more interactive and funny in person than on Skype.

Interestingly, several of them commented that they found me to be more serious in person than on Skype.

17. Janet Schiff (personal communication) has pointed out that this same phenomenon, when it occurs during in-person teaching and supervision, seems stimulated by the nature of the material being discussed.

18. I have disguised the name of the therapist and the patient, but the material is verbatim.

19. This is a volatile subject. In some Western countries such as Italy and Belgium, the wearing of burqas is forbidden by law (France24, 2010), whereas they are a staple of women's dress in some Muslim countries. At *Leucate Plage* (Leucate Plage Nude Beach, 2010) on the Mediterranean coast of France, nude sunbathing is legal, whereas it is illegal in Virginia Beach where I live. The question of how much of a woman's body can be displayed, and under what conditions, seems to be a perennial, polarizing issue.

20. Massively Multiplayer Online Role-Playing Games.

21. For example, see NaDa vs sAviOr @ Shinhan Masters Finals (Game 4), 2007.

Chapter Ten

The Multiple Meanings of the Electrified Mind

Ann G. Smolen

The 41st Annual Margret S. Mahler Symposium on Child Development with its topic "The Electrified Mind," could not be more timely. As we enter the second decade of the twenty-first century, psychoanalysts and psychotherapists are forced to wonder about and address the effect of the numerous uses of the Internet by patients and its use and/or intrusion into the therapeutic relationship. Many questions come to mind concerning technique as the ever widening "analytic frame" must make room for cyberspace and the multiple meanings contained therein. For example, it is not uncommon for therapists to communicate via e-mail with patients. Does this mean that the analyst is now readily and always available? There can be propinquity in e-mail communication. If the analyst does not respond or does so sparingly, narcissistic wounds may be easily incurred. Some analysts find e-mail extremely helpful in staying in contact with a patient over a vacation or in-between sessions if a patient is going through a difficult period. Some may use it to contact a patient for a schedule change. Because e-mail has become commonplace in our lives, we may not think about the deeper meaning that e-mail communication may have such as "the use of passwords and online identities allows for the illusion of a secret, forbidden relationship" (Gabbard 2001, p. 733). Another area to be explored is the confidentiality of e-mail. Psychoanalysis is based on upholding (at all costs) confidentiality. I had an adolescent patient tell me that anything I write and send into cyberspace can be read. The "confidentiality of an e-mail is roughly equivalent to the confidentiality of a postcard" (Gabbard 2001, p. 733). This is a sobering thought.

Online communication has a disinhibiting effect (Gabbard, 2001). I am sure many of us have had the experience of clicking on "send" and wishing

129

we could take it back. As one becomes less inhibited, it seems that impulse control is also affected. As defenses are abandoned, more is revealed than in face-to-face communication. One may easily disclose too much and because the computer serves the purpose of a shield, shame and embarrassment can be avoided (Gabbard, 2001). Is this helpful or a hindrance?

We all know the importance of boundaries within the analytic frame. Cyberspace appears to possess vague, open-ended boundaries. When patients merge cyberspace with analytic space, where are the boundaries? This opens up new possibilities as therapists are forced to redefine boundaries as we grapple with the multiple complex meanings of our patients' use of the Internet. While Freud opened up new ways for people to reflect about themselves, "cybercommunication is expanding the self in new ways" (Gabbard, 2001, p. 734).

Another important area to explore is how the Internet (and text messaging) affects adolescent development. Over the past ten years, I have observed behavior among my patients from age eleven to eighteen that seems very different than in the past. The disinhibiting effect mentioned by Gabbard is quite striking in this age group. I have observed teenagers stealing another's identity in order to hurt that person. Things are said that they would never say in a face-to-face communication and some teens have done things like take seductive photos of themselves and send them out into cyberspace. There is a boldness that occurs. I question whether these behaviors, which are ubiquitous, affect normal development, or whether the conflicts and developmental challenges are the same and technology is just another vehicle through which to express them.

We know that when the child enters adolescence, there is a reappearance of earlier (pre- and post-oedipal) identifications. As the superego develops, a conflict emerges as the adolescent must deal with newfound sexual impulses that need to be contained. While control is needed, the adolescent is in a bind because she/he must also reject external controls by parents and become less dependent. As this is happening, the ego has less support which, in turn, lends itself to a feeling of loneliness and isolation (Rosenblum et al., 1999; Barrett, 2008). The adolescents whom we see in our treatment rooms are often unable to tolerate this phase of development; many turn to cyberspace in order to defend against what is felt as an intolerable emptiness/loneliness. I wonder if this dependence on the Internet stalls growth and does not allow the adolescent to move through this vital developmental phase. I also question if the use of the Internet for this purpose is no different than other defensive behaviors such as binge drinking or drug use.

JOANNE CANTOR'S CONTRIBUTION

Dr. Cantor has studied the impact of the media on children for the past forty years. She also has written books for both children and parents on the subject and brings an extra-analytic view which includes hard data from scientific studies. Dr. Cantor focuses on five points: (1) data on adolescent use of media including ways this has changed over the last decade, (2) the influence of violence in the media on fear and aggression, (3) gaining a better understanding through findings in neurophysiology, (4) the results of research on the impact of multitasking and, (5) guidelines for parents and therapists.

Dr. Cantor takes us back in time, reminding us that whenever a new technology is born, we worry about its impact on our children's behavior and developmental growth. Our grandparents worried about the radio, our parents worried about television and "rock and roll," we worry about cyberspace, text messaging and even "sext" messaging. Ever since American families brought television into their living rooms, researchers have been interested in and concerned about the effect of movies and television on violence and aggression. Dr. Cantor looks back on studies which explore media violence effects to emphasize other effects the media has on children. She is most concerned about the increase in hostility and fears that many children demonstrate from watching violent television and movies. She also cites social learning and imitation as the obvious ways in which watching violence contributes to aggressive and hostile behaviors. She gives a striking example of this phenomenon when Israeli children were exposed to wrestling on television and imitated aggressive behaviors with peers in school. Dr. Cantor weaves the past into the present, bringing us out of memory lane, leaving the clunky console television behind. She states: "If your kids are awake, they are online." The statistics are staggering as we realize that adolescents spend the majority of their awake time either online or text messaging.

In the last ten to twenty years, there have been monumental advances in technology. Gone are the days when families sat down together to watch *Lassie* or *Father Knows Best*. Adolescents have easy access to all forms of media outside of parental eyes/control. Dr. Cantor tells us that over 70 percent of teens have a television in their rooms and even five-year-olds are asking for cellphones. Dr. Cantor's main concern as children are immersed in the Internet, video games, and television are unhealthy outcomes such as higher levels of hostility, a desensitization to violent acts (decreased capacity for empathy?) and increased fears. These outcomes are then associated with interpersonal interactions and how children relate to others influencing all relationships.

Dr. Cantor's paper nicely connects contemporary neurophysiology research data to add relevance to the staggering statistical numbers she presents. She is especially interested in the role of mirror neurons which seem to play a role in imitative behaviors, citing the groundbreaking research in Italy by Iacoboni and his team. She stresses that our brain absorbs what we see, leaving physical residue. Dr. Cantor explains that mirror neurons fire both when we perform an action *and* when we watch someone perform an action. She further states that the more neurons fire, the stronger they become, which means that when a child repeatedly watches violence, mirror neurons are encouraged to fire over and over. Dr. Cantor cites a study where children were shown a picture of a child throwing a ball and the ball hits another child. They were asked what the intention of the thrower was. The children who had just watched a violent video more often answered that the boy intended to hurt the child, whereas the children who had not watched the violent video were less likely to interpret the act as hostile and aggressive. It is my understanding that mirror neurons are involved in reading "intention." Does this mean that watching violence influences interpretation of intent?

Dr. Cantor also explores the neurophysiology of "fear," reminding us that fear was and is important to our evolution and survival as a species. She cites LeDoux's research (1996) demonstrating that fear serves two purposes: (1) we must be quick to get away from the predator, and (2) we must retain a long-term memory of the incident so the next time we do not get eaten. LeDoux (1996) informs us that we interpret the *fearful* situation in our forebrain, and we react physically (heart rate, muscles, hormones) to the situation through our amygdala. Traumatic memories are stored for life in the amygdala. In addition, when the forebrain and the amygdala disagree, the amygdala always wins. Dr. Cantor makes this important reference to help her readers comprehend why a child may be traumatized by a scary movie and carry that irrational fear well into adulthood, knowing intellectually that the fear is not real, but the body reacting as if it is. She simply states: "What we see on the screen stays in the brain."

Dr. Cantor's fourth point focuses on "multitasking." She cites the Kaiser study (2010), which reports that teens multitask 29 percent of the time that they use media. The more gadgets we have, the more we find that we are proficient at multitasking. Many of us are proud that we are *multitaskers*, thinking that we are being exceptionally productive. Dr. Cantor warns that there is growing support that multitasking is counterproductive. The newest research shows that we are not doing two or more tasks simultaneously: our brains are incapable of that feat. What is actually occurring is that the brain switches back and forth between tasks. When this happens, speed is lost as well as accuracy. Research also demonstrates that young people who study while multitasking (instant messaging for example), do less well in school than individuals who focus on studying only.

Dr. Cantor's final point is to offer guidelines for parents and therapists. First and foremost, she feels young children should have parental involvement: children should not have TVs in their rooms, and shows and video games, as well as use of the Internet, should be monitored. As for teens, she urges parents to keep communication open, and keep the computer in a family space where it is in full view. However, as computers and cell phones get smaller and more advanced, it is almost impossible to really know what your teenager is accessing online.

We cannot go backward in time, nor do we wish to, but we need to be educated and aware of adverse effects of the media on our children in order to better protect them from harm. At the same time, a whole new world has opened up where knowledge is obtainable at the click of the mouse. Because of cyberspace we can no longer feign ignorance.

CHRISTINE KIEFFER'S CONTRIBUTION

Dr. Kieffer explores the impact and meaning of the use of cyberspace on adolescent development from a broad perspective including viewpoints from anthropology, sociology, and psychology. She does this in three ways: (1) a historical overview of the research on the impact of television on children; (2) a literature review on two adolescent developmental challenges—obtaining autonomy and constructing an adult identity; and (3) clinical case vignettes.

Dr. Kieffer's review of the studies done by several researchers on the impact of television viewing on children, emphasizing violent shows and their effect on aggression, complements Dr. Cantor's paper, adding a psychoanalytic perspective to the research data. Especially relevant are the studies that demonstrate that children who watch a lot of television were less able to use their imagination and tended not to read books. Dr. Kieffer asked a thought-provoking question, wondering if the actual structure of imagination was altered, and whether this affected frustration tolerance, emotional-relatedness and self-reflection. This is an excellent question not only about television viewing, but heavy Internet and video game use as well. Dr. Kieffer cites Singer and Singer (2005), who have explored the association between video games, imaginative play, and creativity. They stress the difference between passive television viewing and hands-on video game playing. Many feel that role-playing computer and video games enhance creativity and imagination. The Singers warn that this could be misleading. Several researchers remind us that children need "real" experiences in order for imagination and creativity to flourish. Dr. Kieffer provides a through literature review on the many studies investigating these concerns, however she adds her own worries asking three valid and imperative questions: (1) Are children really playing "dress-up" trying on different roles in interactive cyberspace games? (2) What about face-to-face implicit and sensory cues? (3) What does it mean when your playmate is anonymous? Dr. Kieffer addresses these issues in her vast literature review of the topic, demonstrating that some researchers are concerned that development will be thrown offtrack, while other psychoanalysts claim that development can be restored once treatment has begun and obsessive Internet use can be understood.

Dr. Kieffer provides us with an extensive literature review covering adolescent development that is helpful to her reader. She then focuses on two areas of adolescent development and how the use and/or overuse of cyberspace may complicate navigation through these phases. She begins with the adolescent's pursuit for autonomy. Many parents become upset when their teenagers prefer to spend more time on the computer instant messaging and video chatting with friends than spending time with family. Kieffer points out that many parents blame the Internet for what in reality is a healthy move away from family toward a new autonomous self. In fact, the computer has provided parents access into their teen's private world as they "friend" their child on Facebook, much to the embarrassment of the child. A new term has been given to this phenomenon: "helicopter parents," which is equivalent to the intrusive or overprotective parent.

Dr. Kieffer provides an array of diverse and contemporary ideas from several scholars who challenge Mahler's separation-individuation concepts where "mutual independence" is argued for. The self-psychologists prefer the term "relative autonomy," and expand on Kohut's selfobject needs theory to include "adversarial selfobject needs." Kieffer does a fine job of explaining these different approaches to understanding the adolescent's striving for autonomy.

Dr. Kieffer does an equally fine and complete job describing the second adolescent developmental challenge: adolescent identity. She focuses on Blos' seminal work on this topic connecting Internet activities such as Facebook and MySpace and games such as SIMcity to how teens try on different identities until they find one that is a comfortable fit. Once again, Kieffer provides her reader with an extensive literature review in sections titled "Multiplicity of Identity and a Dissociative Model of the Mind," and "Multiple Selves and Cyberselves." She cites a multitude of scholars including William James (1890); Janet (1925); Ferenczi (1949), Sullivan (1953), Mitchell (1991), Bromberg (1998), as well as several others. Dr. Kieffer weaves all of these concepts and theories into a coherent narrative exploring our "multiple and varied selves."

Within her vast literature review, Dr. Kieffer includes Turkle (2005), a social scientist who studies how the computer shapes personal identity. She points out that there is a perception that when an individual creates an online identity he is escaping "real life." Many scientists feel this is a misconception and that creating different online identities promotes creativity and working through, trying out new and different selves.

Dr. Kieffer's final point in this section of her paper explores the idea that the Internet can provide a sense of community. She shares a personal story of her own childhood, where in her close neighborhood Facebook was not needed to communicate with others. In 2010, in many middle class and upper middle class neighborhoods, children are busy in after school activities every day of the week and have little or no time to just hang out with friends in the neighborhood. In this view, children and teenagers long for a close community and are able to gain this through Internet connections.

Dr. Kieffer's paper comes to life in her clinical presentations where theory is relegated to its proper place hovering above our heads as we become immersed in the innerlives of "Candace/Tiffany" and "Paula." Within the stories of these two young adolescent girls, we are drawn into their painful struggles as they navigate through and begin to build healthy peer relationships while simultaneously testing out multiple selves/identities. Candace, who has trouble developing friends, "practices" being the girl she wishes to be as she invents her online persona, Tiffany. It is a lovely example of working through as she shares her secret cyberspace identity with her analyst. Paula, on the other hand, demonstrates her social difficulties by becoming a bully. Dr. Kieffer makes the excellent point that playground bullies are often children who present with disorganized insecure attachment histories. Underneath the mean, nasty exterior is a lonely child longing for connection. We watch Paula transform from the playground bully in elementary school to a full participant as both bully and victim in a "cyberspace war" when she reaches her teen years.

I enjoyed the clinical examples and was left hungry for more details. Dr. Kieffer demonstrates how Candace transformed cyberspace into a play space, bringing it into the transitional space to share with her analyst. Paula did not seem to convert the Internet into a play space, but used it to substitute for connections with peers, albeit in negative and hurtful interactions. I wonder if cyberspace really played a large part in the working through of this difficult developmental phase in both of these cases. I imagine both girls would have found other ways to form and play with fantasy identities and difficult relationships. In other words, are things really so different in our treatment rooms when it comes to intrapsychic exploration? Maybe with the Internet, communications are faster and bolder, but the results are the same.

Drs. Cantor and Kieffer have provided us with research data and clinical material on how adolescents use cyberspace in both negative and positive ways with both negative and positive effects. It is interesting to note that while new language and skills are required as technology advances, there does not seem to be a tangible affect on adolescent development *per se*. Identities continue to be tried on and discarded as the quest for autonomy is sought. The journey remains perilous and exciting. Cyberspace and cell phones just become another part of the environment that we add into the analytic mix.

PATRICIA GIBBS' CONTRIBUTION

Dr. Gibbs explores unconscious meanings of Internet use and the multiple transferences and countertransferences that occurred in two adult patients' analyses that were shaped by their compulsive use of the Internet. Using her clinical material, Dr. Gibbs explored how her patients experienced the *reality* of the transference while absorbed in *virtual reality* and compared these two realities to the "as-if" nature of the transference. She made three significant claims: (1) patients who are "heavy" users of the Internet demonstrate a need to maintain omnipotent control and use denial as a unifying defensive style; (2) Internet addictions reflect a dyadic pre-oedipal transference, and (3) patients who are engrossed in the Internet are actually attempting to fight against separating from the analyst. The computer thus becomes the perfect mother who is always available to soothe and comfort.

Dr. Gibbs states that there are certain personality traits that individuals who overuse the Internet tend to exhibit. Her short literature review looks at studies that state that heavy Internet use is correlated with people who are shy, depressed, and lonely. From her own clinical experience, Dr. Gibbs concluded that these patients are pre-oedipally organized. She described her patients as having difficulty maintaining the "as if" nature of the transference and were concrete thinkers confusing reality with virtual reality.

Dr. Gibbs invites us into her treatment room where we become intimately involved with Mr. N. and Ms. A., whom she describes as pre-oedipally organized with maternal erotic transferences. Through the clinical material of the analyses of both Mr. N. and Ms. A., we see how cyberspace has essentially changed the way these patients experience their bodies and their selves in relation to an anthropomorphically imbued computer. For both patients, the computer took on a human subjectivity. Dr. Gibbs argued that the Internet for Ms. A. became the perfect, always available mother and for Mr. N., the seductive beautiful woman. Both were transference displacements and in both cases the intense Internet involvement caused a detachment in the direct experience with the analyst. It seems that both Ms. A. and Mr. N. have blurred the boundaries between inanimate object and their analyst. Both express longing for human connection and sexuality onto the inanimate computer. Mr. N.'s sexual relationship with the beautiful woman in cyberspace is overt, while Ms. A. only alludes to her sexual feelings when she tells her analyst she masturbates late at night after hours of being online.

Dr. Gibbs demonstrated how her patients projected their "loss of reality" onto her and into their treatments. It is interesting to consider how one's sense of reality is affected by the immediacy of the response via cyberspace. What does it mean to have your object instantaneously available yet physically absent? Perhaps the attachment and the transference are not to the virtual object within cyberspace, but are to the computer itself. Dr. Gibbs stated that her patients were unable to separate from the symbiotic mother/analyst, and it was this inability to tolerate and mourn separation that was the catalyst for displacing the transference onto the virtual object.

Dr. Gibbs concludes her paper, referring to what she calls "ordinary everyday psychosis." She deduces that patients who fuse reality with virtual reality do so as a resistance to experiencing the transference. She states that this phenomenon serves the same purpose as hallucinations, describing how in this process conflicts are distorted and changed into perceptions. Dr. Gibbs states that this took place in both Ms. A. and Mr. N., where verbalization and affect were compromised. For these patients, cyberspace represented an inner world of safety where, in Dr. Gibbs' formulation, Ms. A. and Mr. N. maintained pre-oedipal and maternal erotic transferences. In both of these cases, the "as if" feature of the analytic relationship was unattainable, as it was felt to be too dangerous and too real. Dr. Gibbs explains that cyberspace provided a safe place for sadistic and erotic feelings to emerge.

LANA FISHKIN'S AND RALPH FISHKIN'S CONTRIBUTION

A few years ago, the idea of a "picture phone" was thought of as futuristic, imagined only in movies and fantasy novels. What was once fantastical has now become commonplace. Drs. Cantor, Kieffer, and Gibbs described how children, adolescents, and adults use computers to video-message. My colleagues who are grandparents use Skype to stay in touch with grandchildren who live far away. I have heard stories of young babies under one-year-old kissing the computer screen when Grandmom signs on. Psychoanalysis refuses to be left behind and has entered the electronic age as conducting treatment via Skype has been added to the repertoire. The widening scope now encompasses the "electronic couch" and reaches across the globe. In their paper, the Drs. Fishkin describe their experience using Skype to conduct psychoanalysis and psychotherapy with individuals living in China.

A history of the program is provided, stating that Elise Snyder, M.D., began the Chinese American Psychoanalytic Alliance (CAPA) in 2005; currently forty patients are in psychoanalysis and thirty more are involved in psychodynamic psychotherapy. Both Dr. L. Fishkin and Dr. R. Fishkin supplied clinical material describing their Skype cases. As I read the clinical material, I had to remind myself that these analytic cases were being conducted via Skype. As Dr. R. Fishkin stated, unless you are told you would not know that the analyst and analysand are not together in the same room, but are actually oceans apart. The Fishkins note that the IPA states that a period of face-to-face analysis, in order to establish an analytic process, is essential before embarking on a Skype analysis. Obviously, in these cases, this was impossible, however, both Drs. Fishkin demonstrated that this factor did not derail the treatment, nor did it prevent an analytic process from forming.

The Fishkins had the opportunity to travel to China and meet their patients in person, and they each had very different experiences. Dr. L. Fishkin had a positive experience with her patient. They seemed relaxed and at home with each other, further demonstrating that the use of the computer and geographical distance did not seem to make a difference to their relationship. Dr. R. Fishkin did not describe the meeting in person as a relaxed, positive experience; but both the analyst and analysand found it to be pleasant but unproductive. R. Fishkin cites Akhtar's (2010) understanding and explaining of this uncomfortable face-to-face encounter, making use of the concept of the *waking screen*. Within this concept the computer screen became the vehicle through which this analytic dyad interacted and experienced one another. When the computer screen was removed, and they met in person, both the analyst and analysand relied on defensive postures to deal with this disruption. However, this in-person meeting did not damage the treatment as both analyst and analysand easily resumed their analytic work via Skype.

The Fishkins' touch on the topic of "virtual boundaries," pointing out that boundary crossings become secret and unknown by the other when, for example, either the analyst or analysand may "touch" the image of the other on the computer screen using the cursor. This is certainly fascinating to think about. I also wonder about the room each is in. Does the analyst always Skype from his or her office? Or if it is very early in the morning or very late at night (due to time differences) is the analyst in his/her home? What about the analysands? Do they Skype from the privacy of their bedroom, or even from their bed? As the Fishkins stated, fantasies may be stimulated by these experiences, but it is unclear if the use of the computer intensifies fantasies or "merely objectifies and clarifies their existence." I look forward to reading more about analytic treatments being conducted via Skype as the multiple meanings of the use of the computer come to light. Meanwhile, how wonderful that clinicians in China are able to take part in such an important part of their education with such accomplished analysts.

CONCLUSION

It is often noted with a deep sigh that we have become a "quick fix" society where instant gratification is expected. This "quick fix" trend has had a negative effect on long-term psychodynamic therapies. There is a heavy focus on medication in psychiatric residency programs and short-term cognitive-behavioral therapies are popular. Many patients enter therapy expecting to be "fixed" quickly, and when that does not happen, they ask for medication, thinking that will be the magic bullet. It is not surprising that the Internet seduces us when we are offered quick Internet searches and almost instantaneous connections with others through instant messaging, Facebook, and blogging, not to mention text messaging and Twittering. Given all of the stimulating technology in our everyday lives, it is no wonder that many children have difficulty playing make-believe, or have no desire to find a cozy corner in which to curl up and read a good book or just plain daydream. Current research data makes evident that when children are encouraged and supported in developing fantasy play, they are "more creative, better at problem solving, more resourceful, less aggressive, and better behaved in school" (Blumenthal, 2009, p. 258). There is a disagreement between those who feel that creative, imaginative play is thwarted by video and computer games and those who feel that many of these games actually facilitate imagination and identity formation. One particular study found that "children who played violent games were more likely to show angry thoughts, express beliefs of a hostile nature, show more physiological arousal, demonstrate more overt aggressive behavior, and be less willing to cooperate with or help others" (Bushman and Anderson, 2001).

There is one area that was not addressed that I feel deserves some thought: does the use of BlackBerries, iPhones, and computers have an effect on the relationship and possibly the quality of the attachment between a mother and her infant or young child? It is rather disturbing to observe mothers (fathers and nannies too!) ignoring the demands of their young children because the adult is seemingly engrossed in an electronic device. A patient of mine recently told me an interesting story. Her three-year-old son had two other little boys over for a play date. As the three boys sat enjoying their snack she overheard the following conversation:

Boy #1: "My mommy is always writing papers on the computer."

Boy #2: "My mommy too. She is always looking at the computer."

Boy# 3: "My mommy never stops writing on her computer."

She was struck by this little exchange, but realized that the computer can and does get in the way of being with one's child.

There is much we can find wrong or problematic with our advanced technology and a lot that is positive and useful; however, all of the authors in this conference agree that the Internet is here to stay, as are cell phones and iPhones and iPads. Technology will continue to expand and psychoanalysts will continue to explore the multiple meanings of the electrified mind.

References

Abraham, K. (1911). Giovanni Segantini: a psycho-analytic study. In: *Clinical Papers and Essays by Karl Abraham*, pp. 210–61. London, UK: Hogarth, 1955.

Akhtar, S. (1992). Tethers, orbits, and invisible fences: clinical, developmental, sociocultural, and technical aspects of optimal distance. In: *When the Body Speaks: Psychological Meanings in Kinetic Clues*. eds. S. Kramer and S. Akhtar, pp. 21–57. Northvale, NJ: Jason Aronson.

———. (2005). ed. *Freud along the Ganges: Psychoanalytic Reflections on the People and Culture of India*. New York, NY: Other Press.

———. (2006). Technical challenges faced by the immigrant psychoanalyst. *Psychoanalytic Quarterly* 75: 21–43.

———. (2007). The "listening cure": an overview. In: *Listening to Others: Developmental and Clinical Aspects of Empathy and Attunement*. ed. S. Akhtar, pp. 1–16. Lanham, MD: Jason Aronson.

———. (2009). *Comprehensive Dictionary of Psychoanalysis*. London, UK: Karnac Books.

———. (2009). Waking screen. In: *Comprehensive Dictionary of Psychoanalysis*, p. 306. London, UK: Karnac Books.

———. (2010). Discussion at the 41st Annual Margaret S. Mahler Symposium titled "The Electrified Mind: Development, Psychopathology, and Treatment in the Era of Cell Phones and the Internet." Philadelphia, PA, April 10, 2010.

Amati-Mehler, J., Argentieri, S., and Canestri, J. (1993). *The Babel of the Unconscious: Mother Tongue and Foreign Languages in the Psychoanalytic Dimension*. New York, NY: International Universities Press.

Anderson, C. A. (2004). An update on the effects of playing violent video games. *Journal of Adolescence* 27: 113–22.

Anderson, C. A., and Bushman, B.J. (2001). Effects of violent video games on aggressive behavior, aggressive cognition, aggressive affect, physiological arousal, and prosocial behavior: a meta-analytic review of the scientific literature. *Psychological Science* 12: 353–59.

Arieti, S. (1974). The cognitive transformation. In: *Interpretation of Schizophrenia*, pp. 224–302. New York, NY: Basic Books.

Arlow, J. (1980). The revenge motive in the primal scene. *Journal of the American Psychoanalytic Association* 28: 519–41.

Aron, L., and Harris, A. (1993). eds. *The Legacy of Sandor Ferenczi*. Hillsdale, NJ: Analytic Press.

Aronson, S., Scheidlinger, S., and Hajal, F. (2003). eds. *Group Treatment of Adolescents in Context: Outpatient, Inpatient, and School*. New York, NY: International Universities Press.

"Author's name withheld by request" (2008). Exporting psychoanalysis to mainland China? *The American Psychoanalyst* 42: 10–11.

Balint, M. (1969). *The Basic Fault*. Evanston, IL: Northwestern University Press, 1992.

Barrett, T. F. (2008). Manic defenses against loneliness in adolescence. *The Psychoanalytic Study of the Child* 63: 111–36.

BBC News. (2002). Is porn good for society? May 14. http://news.bbc.co.uk/2/hi/uk_news/1986869.stm.

Benjamin, J. (2004). The analytic third: beyond doer and done-to. *Psychoanalytic Quarterly* 73: 5–46.

Benson, R. (2005). Personal Communication.

Berson, T. (2010). Personal communication.

Bick, E. (1968). The experience of the skin in early object relations. *International Journal of Psychoanalysis* 49: 484–86.

Big Pond News (2010). Medical students to use *Second Life*. May 12, 2010. http://bigpond-news.com/articles/Technology/2010/05/12/Medical_students_to_use_Second_Life_461015.html.

Bion, W. R. (1956) Development of schizophrenic thought. In: *W. R. Bion Second Thoughts*, pp. 36–42. London, UK: Karnac, 1984.

———. (1957). Differentiation of the psychotic from the non-psychotic personalities. *International Journal of Psychoanalysis* 38: 266–75.

———. (1961). *Experiences in Groups and Other Papers*. New York, NY: Brunner-Routledge.

———. (1962). A theory of thinking. In: *W. R. Bion Second Thoughts*, pp. 110–19. London, UK: Karnac, 1984.

Black, S. L., and Bevan, S. (1992). At the movies with Buss and Durkee: a natural experiment on film violence. *Aggressive Behavior* 18: 37–45.

Blackman, J. (2001). On childless stepparents. In: *Stepparenting: Creating and Recreating Families in America Today*. eds. S. Cath and M. Shopper, pp. 168–82. Hillsdale, NJ: Analytic Press.

———. (2003). *101 Defenses: How the Mind Shields Itself*. New York, NY: Brunner-Routledge.

———. (2010). *Get the Diagnosis Right: Assessment and Treatment Selection for Mental Disorders*. New York, NY: Routledge.

Blos, P. (1960). *On Adolescence*. New York, NY: International Universities Press.

———. (1962). *On Adolescence: A Psychoanalytic Interpretation*. New York, NY: Free Press.

———. (1967). The second individuation process of adolescence. *Psychoanalytic Study of the Child* 22: 162–86.

———. (1968). Character formation in adolescence. *Psychoanalytic Study of the Child* 23: 245–63.

Blumer, H. (1933). *Movies and Conduct*. New York, NY: Macmillan.

Boellstorf, T. (2008). *Coming of Age in Second Life: An Anthropologist Explores the Virtually Human*. Princeton, NJ: Princeton University Press.

Boesky, D. (1982). Acting out: a reconsideration of the concept. *International Journal of Psychoanalysis* 63: 39–55.

Bowlby John, (1952). Maternal care and mental health. (WHO) *Monograph Series No. 2*, p. 11. Geneva, Switzerland.

Boyer, L.B. (2000). *Countertransference and Regression*. Northvale, NJ: Jason Aronson.

Brazelton, T. (1992). *Touchpoints: Your Child's Emotional and Behavioral Development, Birth to 3—The Essential Reference for the Early Years*. Cambridge, MA: DaCapo Lifelong Books.

Bretherton, I. (1992). The origins of attachment theory: John Bowlby and Mary Ainsworth. *Developmental Psychology* 28: 759–75. http://www.psychology.sunysb.-edu/attachment/online/inge_origins.pdf.

Brigham Young University National Pornography Statistics. *BYU Women's Services*. http://wsr.byu.edu/content/national-pornography-statistics.

Bromberg, P. (1998). *Standing in the Spaces: Essays on Clinical Process, Trauma and Dissociation.* Hillsdale, NJ: Analytic Press.

Brown, S. (2003). *Hello, Darkness.* New York, NY: Simon and Schuster.

Buckley, C. (1-1-2010). China says 5,394 arrested in internet porn crackdown. *Reuters.* http://www.reuters.com/article/idUSTRE60004220100101.

Buie, D. (1981). Empathy: its nature and limitations. *Journal of the American Psychoanalytic Association* 29: 281–307.

Bushman, B. J., and Anderson, C. A. (2001). Media violence and the American public: scientific facts versus media misinformation. *American Psychologist* 56: 477–89.

Bushman, B. J., and Cantor, J. (2003). Media ratings for violence and sex: implications for policy makers and parents. *American Psychologist* 58: 130–41.

Cambridge Women's Pornography Cooperative and Anderson, S. (2007). *Porn for Women.* San Francisco, CA: Chronicle Books.

Cantor, J. (1998). *"Mommy, I'm Scared": How TV and Movies Frighten Children and What We Can Do to Protect Them.* San Diego, CA: Harvest/Harcourt.

———. (2009). *Conquer CyberOverload: Get More Done, Boost Your Creativity, and Reduce Stress.* Madison, WI: CyberOutlook Press.

———. (2009). Fright reactions to mass media. In: *Media Effects: Advances in Theory and Research.* eds. J. Bryant and M. B. Oliver, pp. 287–303. New York, NY: Routledge.

Chak, K. (2004). Shyness and locus of control as predictors of internet addiction and internet use. *Cyberpsychological Behavior* 7: 559–70.

Chakroff, J. L., and Nathanson, A. I. (2008). Parent and school interventions: mediation and media literacy. In: *The Handbook of Children, Media, and Development.* eds. S. L. Calvert and B. J. Wilson, pp. 552–76. Malden, MA: Blackwell Publishing.

Chused, J. F. (1991). The evocative power of enactments. *Journal of the American Psychoanalytic Association* 39: 615–40.

Cline, V. B., Croft, R. G., and Courrier, S. (1973). Desensitization of children to television violence. *Journal of Personality and Social Psychology* 27: 360–65.

Coates, S., Friedman, R., and Wolfe, S. (1991). The etiology of boyhood gender identity disorder: a model for integrating temperament, development, and psychodynamics. *Psychoanalytic Dialogues* 1: 481–523.

Cramer-Azima, F., and Richmond, L. (2003). *Adolescent Group Psychotherapy.* New York, NY: International Universities Press.

Daly, R. (2010). States address diverse issues affecting mental health care. *Psychiatric News,* p. 6. April 2, 2010.

Davies, J. M. (1994). Desire and dread in the analyst: Reply to Glen Gabbard's commentary on "Love in the Afternoon." *Psychoanalytic Dialogues* 4: 503–8.

Davies, J. M., and Frawley, M-G (1994). *Treating the Adult Survivor of Sexual Abuse.* New York, NY: Basic Books.

Dini, K. (2008). *Video Games: Play and Addiction.* New York, NY: iUniverse, Inc.

———. (2009). Panel report: internet interaction—the effects on patients' lives and the analytic process. *Journal of the American Psychoanalytic Association* 57: 979–98.

———. (2010). On video games, culture and therapy. *Psychoanalytic Inquiry:* in press.

Dworkin, A. (1981). *Men and Boys.* Chapter 2 Pornography: Men Possessing Women. http://www.nostatusquo.com/ACLU/dworkin/PornMenandBoys1.html.

Dysinger, W. S., and Ruckmick, C. A. (1933). *The Emotional Responses of Children to the Motion Picture Situation.* New York, NY: Macmillan.

Earth Station. *World's Fair and Exposition Information and Conference Guide; 1964–65 New York World's Fair.* http://www.earthstation9.com/1964_new1.htm.

Edgcumbe, R. (1984). Modes of communication: the differentiation of somatic and verbal expression. *Psychoanalytic Study of the Child* 39: 137–54.

Eigen, M. (2001). *Damaged Bonds.* London, UK: Karnac.

Eisenberg, A. (1936). *Children and Radio Programs.* New York, NY: Columbia University Press.

Engelberg, E., and Sjoberg, L. (2004). Internet use, social skills, and adjustment. *Cyberpsychological Behavior* 7:41–47.

Erikson, E. (1950). *Childhood and Society.* New York, NY: W. W. Norton, 1963.

Essig, T. (2010). Psychoanalysis—lost but not in cyber-space. *Psychoanalytic Inquiry:* in press.

Fackler, M. (2007). In Korea, a boot camp for web obsession. *New York Times, Technology,* Page 1, November 18, 2007. http://www.nytimes.com/2007/11/18/technology/18rehab.html?_r=1andpagewanted=1andr=2.

Fairbairn, W. R. D. (1951). A synopsis of the author's views regarding the structure of the personality. In: *Psychoanalytic Studies of the Personality,* pp. 162–79. Boston, MA: Routledge and Kegan Paul, 1952.

Family Safe Media (2006). *Pornography Statistics.* http://www.familysafemedia.com/pornography_statistics.html

Ferenczi, S. (1949). Confusion of tongues between the adult and the child. *International Journal of Psychoanalysis* 30: 225–31.

———. (1916). Stages in the Development of the Sense of Reality. In: *Sex in Psychoanalysis,* pp. 213–39. New York, NY: Robert Brunner, 1950.

Foerde, K., Knowlton, B., and Poldrack, R. A. (2006). Modulation of competing memory systems by distraction. *Proceedings of the National Academy of Sciences.* www.pnas.org/cgi/doi/10.1073/pnas.0602659103

Fonagy, P. (2001). *Attachment Theory and Psychoanalysis.* New York, NY: Other Press.

———. (1998). An attachment theory approach to treatment of the difficult patient. *Bulletin of the Menninger Clinic* 62: 147–69.

Fonagy, P., Steele, M., Moran, G., Steele, H., and Higgitt, A. (1993). Measuring the ghost in the nursery: an empirical study of the relation between parents' mental representations of childhood experiences and their infants' security of attachment. *Journal of the American Psychoanalytic Association* 41: 957–89.

Fong, V. (2007). Parent-child communication problems and the perceived inadequacies of Chinese only-children. *Ethos* 35: 85–127.

France24 (2010). The burqa, the law and other EU countries. Jan. 26, 2010. http://www.france24.com/en/20100126-burqa-law-other-eu-countries.

Freud, A. (1936). *The Ego and the Mechanisms of Defense.* New York, NY: International Universities Press, 1966.

———. (1958). *The Writings of Anna Freud, V. 5,* pp. 136–66, New York, NY: International Universities Press.

———. (1965). *Normality and Pathology in Pathology and Childhood.* New York, NY: International Universities Press

Freud, S. (1893). On the psychical mechanism of hysterical phenomena: a lecture. *Standard Edition* 3: 25–41.

———. (1919). A child is being beaten: a contribution to the study of the origin of sexual perversions. *Standard Edition* 17: 175–204.

———. (1920). Beyond the pleasure principle. *Standard Edition* 18: 7–65.

———. (1923). The ego and the id. *Standard Edition* 19: 3–68.

———. (1930). Civilization and its discontents. *Standard Edition* 21: 57–146.

Fried, C. B. (2008). In-class laptop use and its effects on student learning. *Computers and Education* 50: 906–14.

Friedman, L. (2005). Flirting with virtual reality. *Psychoanalytic Quarterly* 74: 639–60.

Gabbard, G. (1994). Sexual excitement and countertransference love in the analyst. *Journal of the American Psychoanalytic Association* 42: 1083–1106.

———. (2001). Cyberpassion: e-rotic transference on the internet, *Psychoanalytic Quarterly* 70: 719–38.

———. (2009). The decline and fall of analytic anonymity. Presented at the *International Psychoanalytic Association Conference,* July 31, 2009.

Galatzer-Levy, R. M. (2002). Emergence. *Psychoanalytic Inquiry* 22: 708–27.

Galatzer-Levy, R., and Cohler, B. J. (1993). *The Essential Other: A Developmental Psychology of the Self.* New York, NY: Basic Books

———. (2010). Obscuring desire: a special pattern of male adolescent masturbation, internet pornography, and the flight from meaning. *Psychoanalytic Inquiry:* in press.

Gentile, D. A., and Walsh, D.A. (1999). *MediaQuotient(tm) : National Survey of Family Media Habits, Knowledge, and Attitudes.* Minneapolis, MN: National Institute on Media and the Family.

Gibbs, P. L. (2004). The struggle to know what is real. *Psychoanalytic Review* 91: 615–41.

———. (2007a). Reality in cyberspace: analysands' use of the Internet and ordinary everyday psychosis. *Psychoanalytic Review* 94: 11–38.

———. (2007b). The primacy of psychoanalytic intervention in recovery from the psychoses and schizophrenias. *Journal of the American Academy of Psychoanalysis and Dynamic Psychiatry* 35: 287–312.

———. (2009). Technical challenges in the psychoanalytic treatment of psychotic depression. In: *Beyond Medication: Therapeutic Engagement and Recovery from Psychosis.* eds. D. Garfield and D. Mackler, pp. 79–83. London, UK: Routledge.

Gilbert, C. (1982). *In a Different Voice: Psychological Theory and Women's Development.* Cambridge, MA: Harvard University Press.

Goldberger, M. (1988). The two-man phenomenon. *Psychoanalytic Quarterly* 57: 229–33.

Goldstein, J., ed. (1998). *Why We Watch: The Attractions of Violent Entertainment.* New York, NY: Oxford University Press.

Grotstein, J. (1990). Nothingness, meaninglessness, chaos, and the "black hole," II. *Contemporary Psychoanalysis* 26: 377–407.

Halberstadt-Freud, H. C. (1998). Electra versus Oedipus: femininity reconsidered. *International Journal of Psychoanalysis* 79: 41–56.

Hand, B. *AT&T introduces Picturephone, the first video conference system, at the New York World's Fair.* http://www.timelines.com/1964/4/22/at-t-introduces-the-first-video-conference-system-at-the-new-york-worlds-fair.

Hanlon, J. (2001). Disembodied intimacies: identity and relationship on the Internet. *Psychoanalytic Psychology* 18: 566–71.

Harlow, H. (1958). The nature of love. *American Psychologist* 13: 673–78.

Harris, A. (2005). *Gender as Soft Assembly.* Hillsdale, NJ: Analytic Press.

Harrison, K., and Cantor, J. (1999). Tales from the screen: enduring fright reactions to scary media. *Media Psychology* 1: 97–116.

Hartman, S. (2010). Mourning and cyberspace?? *Psychoanalytic Inquiry*: in press.

Heim, M. (1993). *The Metaphysics of Virtual Reality.* Oxford, UK: Oxford University Press.

Herzog, J. M. (1980). Sleep disturbance and father hunger in 18- to 28-month-old boys: the Erlkonig syndrome. *Psychoanalytic Study of the Child* 35: 219–23.

———. (2004). Father hunger and narcissistic deformation. *Psychoanalytic Quarterly* 73: 893–914.

Hoekstra, S. J., Harris, R. J., and Helmick, A. L. (1999). Autobiographical memories about the experience of seeing frightening movies in childhood. *Media Psychology* 1: 117–40.

Howell, E. F. (2005). *The Dissociative Mind.* Hillsdale, NJ: Analytic Press.

Huesmann, L. R. (1986). Psychological processes promoting the relation between exposure to media violence and aggressive behavior by the viewer. *Journal of Social Issues* 42: 125–40.

Huesmann, L. R. and Eron, L. (1986). *Television and the Aggressive Child: A Cross-National Comparison.* Hillsdale, NJ: Lawrence Erlbaum Associates.

Huffstutter, P. (2007). Frontier justice in an online world? *Seattle Times,* November 23, 2007. http://seattletimes.nwsource.com/html/nationworld/2004030463_suicide23.html.

Iacoboni, M. (2008). *Mirroring People: The New Science of How We Connect with Others.* New York, NY: Farrar, Straus and Giroux.

In Her Shoes. (2005). http://www.imdb.com/title/tt1388125/

Innes-Smith, J. (1987). Pre-oedipal identification and the cathexis of autistic objects in the aetiology of adult psychopathology. *International Journal of Psychoanalysis* 68: 405–13.

Itzkoff, D. (2010). Infernal videogame redoes Dante. *Philadelphia Inquirer,* pp. W-19-20, February 5, 2010.

Jackson, M. (2009). *Distracted: the Erosion of Attention and The Coming Dark Age.* Amherst, NY: Prometheus Books.

Jaffe, C. (2000). Organizing adolescent(ce): a dynamic systems perspective on adolescence and adolescent psychotherapy, *Adolescent Psychiatry* 25: 17–43.

James, W. (1890). *The Principles of Psychology.* Boston, MA: Harvard University Press, 1983.

Janet, P. (1925). *Psychological Healing, Volume 1.* New York, NY: Macmillan.

Joseph, B. (1987). Projective identification: some clinical aspects. In: *Psychic Equilibrium and Psychic Change: Selected Papers of Betty Joseph.* eds. M. Feldman and E. B. Spillius. London, UK: Routledge, 1989.

Josephine Earp (2010). Wikepedia.com. http://en.wikipedia.org/wiki/Josephine_Earp.

Kaiser Family Foundation (2010). Generation M^2: media in the lives of 8- to 18-year-olds. Report presented at the *Program for the Study of Media and Health Forum*, Washington, DC. January 20, 2010.

Kaplan, L. (1984). *Adolescence: The Farewell to Childhood.* New York, NY: Simon and Schuster.

Kaplan, R. B. (1965). Reflections regarding psychomotor activities during the latency period. *Psychoanalytic Study of the Child* 20: 220–38.

Katan, A. (1961). Some thoughts about the role of verbalization in early childhood. *Psychoanalytic Study of the Child* 16: 184–88.

Kernberg, O. (1980). Developmental theory, structural organization, and psychoanalytic technique. In: *Rapprochement: The Critical Subphase of Separation-Individuation.* eds. R. Lax, S. Bach, and J. Beuland, pp. 23–28. New York, NY: Jason Aronson,

Kieffer, C.C. (2007). Emergence and the analytic third: working on the edge of chaos. *Psychoanalytic Dialogues* 17: 683–704.

———. (2010). Adolescence as a time to play. In: *Play and Playfulness.* ed. M. Akhtar. Lanham, MD: Jason Aronson.

Kirsh, S. J. (1998). Seeing the world through Mortal Kombat-colored glasses: violent video games and the development of a short-term hostile attribution bias. *Childhood* 5: 177–84.

Kleeman, J. A. (1976). Freud's views on early female sexuality in the light of direct child observation. *Journal of the American Psychoanalytic Association* 24S: 3–26.

Klein, M. (1945). The Oedipus complex in light of early anxieties. *International Journal of Psychoanalysis* 26: 11–33.

———. (1946). Notes on some schizoid mechanisms. *International Journal of Psychoanalysis* 27: 99–110.

Klein, S. (1980). Autistic phenomena in neurotic patients. *International Journal of Psychoanalysis* 61: 395–402.

Klingberg, T. (2009). *The Overflowing Brain: Information Overload and the Limits of Working Memory.* trans. N. Betteridge. London, UK: Oxford University Press.

Knight, R. (2005). The process of attachment and autonomy in latency: a longitudinal study of 10 children. *Psychoanalytic Study of the Child* 60: 178–210.

Knocked Up (2007). http://www.imdb.com/title/tt0478311/.

Kogan, I. (1999). The immigrant patient and the analyst of the same descent. Presented at Brixen, Italy, July 23.

Kohlberg, L. (1981). *The Philosophy of Moral Development.* San Francisco, CA: Harper and Row.

Kohut, H. (1971). *Analysis of the Self.* New York, NY: International Universities Press.

———. (1977). *The Restoration of the Self.* New York, NY: International Universities Press.

Krystal, H. (1988). *Integration and Self-Healing: Affect, Trauma, Alexithymia.* Hillsdale, NJ: Analytic Press.

Kumin, I. (1985–1986). Erotic horror: desire and resistance in the psychoanalytic situation. *International Journal of Psychoanalytic Psychotherapy* 11: 3–20.

La Farge, L. (1989). Emptiness as defense in severe regressive states. *Journal of the American Psychoanalytic Association* 47: 965–95.

LaSpina, J. A. (1998). *The Visual Turn and the Transformation of the Textbook.* Mahwah, NJ: Lawrence Erlbaum Associates.

Laufer, M. (1976). The central masturbation fantasy, the final sexual organization, and adolescence. *Psychoanalytic Study of the Child* 31: 297–316.

LeDoux, J. (1996). *The Emotional Brain: The Mysterious Underpinnings of Emotional Life.* New York, NY: Simon and Schuster.

———. (2002). *The Synaptic Self.* New York, NY: Viking Penguin.

Lemish, D. (1997). The school as a wrestling arena: the modeling of a television series. *Communication* 22: 395–418.

Letters to the Editor (2008). *The American Psychoanalyst* 42: 35–38.

Leucate Plage Nude Beach (2010). http://www.nude-france.com/Leucate-Plage.htm.

Levi-Strauss, C. (1963). *Structural Anthropology*. New York, NY: Basic Books.

Lewin, T. (2010). If your kids are awake, they're probably online. *New York Times*, January 20, 2010, available online.

Lewin, V. (2004). *The Twin in the Transference*. London, UK: Whurr Publishers.

Lichtenberg, J., Lachmann, F., and Fosshage, J. (2001). *Self and Motivational Systems: Towards a Theory of Psychoanalytic Technique*. Hillsdale, NJ: Analytic Press.

Lidz, R. (1989). The use of anxiety and hostility in the treatment of schizophrenic patients. In: *Psychoanalysis and Psychosis*. ed. A-L. Silver, pp. 207–19. Madison, CT: International Universities Press.

Liotti, G. (1995). Disoriented/dissociated attachment in the psychotherapy of dissociative disorders. In: *Attachment Theory: Social, Developmental and Clinical Perspectives*. eds. S. Goldberg, R. Moire, and J. Kerr, pp. 343–63. Hillsdale, NJ: Analytic Press.

Litowitz, B. E. (2010). Personal communication, 2/7/10.

Luria, A. R. (1932). *The Nature of Human Conflicts*. New York, NY: Liveright

Lyons-Ruth, K. (2003). Dissociation and the parent-infant dialogue: a longitudinal perspective from attachment research. *Journal of the American Psychoanalytic Association* 51: 883–910.

Mahler, M. S. (1952). On child Psychosis and schizophrenia: autistic and symbiotic infantile psychoses. *Psychoanalytic Study of the Child* 7: 286–305.

———. (1968). *On Human Symbiosis and the Vicissitudes of Individuation*. New York, NY: International Universities Press.

———. (1971). A study of the separation-individuation process and its possible application to borderline phenomena in the psychoanalytic situation. *Psychoanalytic Study Child* 26: 403–24.

Mahler, M., Pine, F., and Bergmann, A. (1975). *The Psychological Birth of a Human Infant*. New York, NY: Basic Books.

Marcus, I. (1980). Harmony vs. discord in marriage: a view of physicians' marriages. *Journal of the Louisiana State Medical Society* 132: 173–78.

Marcus, I. (2004). *Why Men Have Affairs*. Jefferson, LA: Garrity Printing.

Marcus, I., and Francis, J. (1975). Developmental aspects of masturbation. In: *Masturbation from Infancy to Senescence*. eds. I. Marcus and J. Francis. New York, NY: International Universities Press.

Masterson, J. (1975). The splitting mechanism of the borderline adolescent: developmental and clinical aspects. In: *Borderline States in Psychiatry*. ed. J. Mack, pp. 17–32. New York, NY: Grune and Stratton.

McDougall, J. (1989). *Theatres of the Body: A Psychoanalytic Approach to Psychosomatic Illness*. New York, NY: W. W. Norton.

Medina, J. (2008). *Brain Rules: 12 Principles for Surviving and Thriving at Work, Home, and School*. Seattle, WA: Pear Press.

Meers, D. (1975). Masturbation and the ghetto. In: *Masturbation from Infancy to Senescence*. eds. I. Marcus and J. Francis. New York, NY: International Universities Press.

Meltzoff, A. N., and Moore, M. K. (1977). Imitation of facial and manual gestures by human neonates. *Science* 198: 75–78.

Milgram, S. (1963). Behavioral study of obedience. *Journal of Abnormal and Social Psychology* 67: 371–78.

Mitchell, S. A. (1991). *Influence and Autonomy in Psychoanalysis*. Hillsdale, NJ: Analytic Press.

———. (1993). *Hope and Dread in Psychoanalysis*. New York, NY: Basic Books.

Modell, A.H. (1968). *Object Love and Reality*. New York, NY: International Universities Press.

———. (1976). The holding environment and the therapeutic action of psychoanalysis. *Journal of the American Psychoanalytic Association* 24: 285–307.

Molitor, F., and Hirsch, K. W. (1994). Children's toleration of real-life aggression after exposure to media violence: a replication of the Drabman and Thomas studies. *Child Study Journal* 24: 191–207.

Morrison, S. (2009). A second chance for *Second Life*: Northrop, IBM use virtual world as setting for training, employee meetings. *Wall Street Journal*, August 19, 2009, available online.

Mullin, C. R., and Linz, D. (1995). Desensitization and resensitization to violence against women: effects of exposure to sexually violent films on judgments of domestic violence victims. *Journal of Personality and Social Psychology* 69: 449–59.

NaDa vs sAviOr @ Shinhan masters finals (2007). *Starcraft* finals. http://www.youtube.com.

Nalwa, K., and Anand, A. (2003). Internet addiction in students: a cause of concern. *Cyberpsychological Behavior* 6: 653–56.

Nathanson, A. I. (2002). The unintended effects of parental mediation of television on adolescents. *Media Psychology* 4: 207–30.

Nosek, L. (2009). Body and infinite: notes for a theory of genitality. *International Journal of Psychoanalysis* 90: in press.

Ogden, T. (1989). *The Primitive Edge of Experience*. Northvale, NJ: Jason Aronson.

———. (1994). *Subjects of Analysis*. Northvale, NJ: Jason Aronson.

———. (1995). Analyzing forms of aliveness and deadness of the counter-transference/countertransference. *International Journal of Psychoanalysis* 76: 695–710.

Ophir, E., Nass, C., and Wagner, A. D. (2009). Cognitive control in media multitaskers. *Proceedings of the National Academy of Sciences.* www.pnas.org/-cgi/doi/10.1073/pnas.0903620106.

Orange, D., Atwood, G. E. and Stolorow, R. D. (1997). *Working Intersubjectively.* Hillsdale, NJ: Analytic Press.

Orol, R. (2010). SEC staff surfed porn sites during crisis buildup: inspector. *Wall Street Journal, Marketwatch,* April 23, 2010.

Owens, J., Maxim, R., McGuinn, M., Nobile, C., Msall, M., and Alario, A. (1999). Television-viewing habits and sleep disturbance in school children. *Pediatrics* 104: 552–63.

Pacella, B., (1980). The primal matrix configuration. In: *Rapprochement: The Critical Subphase of Separation-Individuation.* eds. R. Lax, S. Bach, and J. A. Burland, pp. 117–31. New York, NY: Jason Aronson.

Paik, H., and Comstock, G. (1994). The effects of television violence on antisocial behavior: a meta-analysis. *Communication Research* 21: 516–46.

Palfrey, J., and Gasser, U. (2008). *Born Digital: Understanding the First Generation of Digital Natives.* New York, NY: Basic Books.

Paniagua, C. (1998). Acting in revisited. *International Journal of Psychoanalysis* 79: 499–512.

———. (2004). *Visiones de España: Reflexiones de un Psicoanalista.* Madrid, Spain: Biblioteca Nueva.

Parens, H., Scattergood, E., Singletary, W., and Duff, A. (1994). *Aggression in Our Children: Coping with It Constructively.* Northvale, NJ: Jason Aronson.

Person, E. S. (1986). Male sexuality and power. *Psychoanalytic Inquiry* 6: 3–25.

Piaget, J. (1937). *The Construction of Reality in the Child.* New York, NY: Basic Books.

Piers, C., Mueller, J. P., and Brent, J. (2007). eds. *Self-organizing Complexity in Psychological Systems (Psychological Issues).* New York, NY: Jason Aronson.

Pojman, A. P. (2009). *Adolescent Group Psychotherapy: Method, Madness and the Basics.* New York, NY: American Group Psychotherapy Association Press.

Provenzano, E. (2003). Virtuous war: simulation and the militarization of play, In: *Education as Enforcement: The Militarization and Corporatization of Schools.* eds. K. J. Saltman and D. A. Gabbard, pp. 279–88. New York, NY: Routledge.

Putnam, F. W. (1997). *Dissociation in Children and Adolescents.* New York, NY: Guilford Press.

Racker, H. (1953). A contribution to the problem of countertransference. *International Journal of Psychoanalysis* 34: 313–24.

Ramachandran, V. S. (2006). *Mirror neurons and the brain in the vat.* http://www.edge.org/3rd_culture/ramachandran06/ramachandran06_index.html

Reik, T. (1951). *Listening with the Third Ear.* Garden City, NY: Garden City Books.

Rexford, E. (1966). *Developmental Approaches to the Problem of Acting Out.* New York, NY: International Universities Press.

Rideout, V., Foehr, U., and Roberts, D. G. (2010). *Generation M2: Media in the lives of 8- to 18-year-olds.* Kaiser Family Foundation. Available at: http://www.kff.org/entmedia/mh012010pkg.cfm

Rosenblum, D. S., Daniolos, P., Kass, N., and Martin, A. (1999). Adolescents and popular culture: a psychodynamic overview. *Psychoanalytic Study of the Child* 54: 319–38.

Roth, J. D., and Kohn, N. V. (2010). The blank screen of cyberspace. *Psychoanalytic Inquiry:* in press.

Sandler, J. (1960). On the concept superego. *Psychoanalytic Study of the Child* 15: 128–62.

Sartre, J. P. (1944). *No Exit. (Huis Clos).* New York, NY: Vintage Books.

Scealy, M., Phillips, J., and Stevenson, R. (2002). Shyness and anxiety as predictors of patterns of Internet usage. *Cyberpsychological Behavior* 5: 507–15.

Schachter, J., and Kaechele, H. (2010). The couch in psychoanalysis. *Contemporary Psychoanalysis,* in press.

Scharff, J. (2009). Telephone analysis. *IPA Electronic Newsletter* (December 8, 2009).

Schmohl, P. (2010). *Worldgate's next big thing: Ojo video phone and telecommunications at lightspeed.* http://www.examiner.com/X-32974-DC-Home-Technology Examiner~y2010m3d5-the-next-big-thing.

Searles, H. F. (1979a). *Countertransference and Related Subjects.* New York, NY: International Universities Press.

———. (1979b). Concerning therapeutic symbiosis: the patient as symbiotic therapist, the phase of ambivalent symbiosis, and the role of jealousy in the fragmented ego. In: *Countertransference and Related Subjects,* pp. 426–87. New York, NY: International Universities Press.

Seligman, S. (2005). Complexity and sensibility: non-linear dynamic systems theory as a meta-framework for psychoanalysis. Presented at the *Division 39 Spring Conference,* New York, NY, April 14, 2005.

Shapiro, T. (1979). *Clinical Psycholinguistics.* New York, NY: Plenum Press.

Shatz, C. (2006). Quotation described in *Harvard Medical Alumni Bulletin.* http://alumnibulletin.med.harvard.edu/discovery/sparks/shatz.php.

Shengold, L. (1985). Defensive anality and anal narcissism. *International Journal of Psychoanalysis* 66: 47–64.

———. (1989). *Soul Murder: The Effect of Childhood Abuse and Deprivation.* New Haven, CT: Yale University Press.

Siegel, D. (1999). *The Developing Mind: Toward a Neurobiology of Interpersonal Experience.* New York, NY: Guilford Press.

Singer, D. G., and Singer, J. L. (2005). *Imagination and Play in the Electronic Age.* Cambridge, MA: Harvard University Press.

Singer, M., I., Slovak, K., Frierson, T., and York, P. (1998). Viewing preferences, symptoms of psychological trauma, and violent behaviors among children who watch television. *Journal of the American Academy of Child and Adolescent Psychiatry* 37: 1041–48.

Skorton, D. (2010). Letter to the editor. *New York Times,* March 23, 2010.

Small, B. (2002). *Rosamund.* London, UK: Penguin Books.

———. (2003). *Until You.* New York, NY: New American Library.

Spitz, R., and Cobliner, W. G. (1966). *The First Year of Life: A Psychoanalytic Study of Normal and Deviant Development of Object Relations.* New York, NY: International Universities Press.

Steiner, J. (1993). *Psychic Retreats: Pathological Organizations in Psychotic, Neurotic and Borderline Patients.* London, UK: Routledge.

Stern, D. (1997). *Unformulated Experience: From Dissociation to Imagination in Psychoanalysis.* Hillsdale, NJ: Analytic Press.

———. (2009). *Partners in Thought: Working with Unformulated Experience, Dissociation and Enactment.* London, UK: Routledge.

Stoller, R. J. (1968). *Sex and Gender: On the Development of Masculinity and Femininity.* New York, NY: Science House.

———. (1985). *Observing the Erotic Imagination.* New Haven, CT: Yale University Press.

Stolorow, R. D. (2007). *Trauma and Human Existence: Autobiographic, Psychoanalytic and Philosophical Reflections.* London, UK: Routledge.

Subrahmanyam, K., Greenfield, P. M., and Tynes, B. (2004). Constructing sexuality and identity in an online teen chat room. *Journal of Applied Developmental Psychology* 25: 651–66.

Suler, J. (2002). The basic psychological features of cyberspace. In: *The Psychology of Cyberspace.* Online hypertext.

———. (2004). The online disinhibition effect. *Cyberpsychology and Behavior* 7: 321–26.

Sullivan, H. S. (1953). *The Interpersonal Theory of Psychiatry.* New York, NY: W. W. Norton.

Sunstein, C. (2009). *On Rumors: How Falsehoods Spread, Why We Believe Them, What Can Be Done.* New York, NY: Farrar, Straus and Giroux.

Tausk, V. (1933). On the origin of the "Influencing Machine" in schizophrenia. *Psychoanalytic Quarterly* 2: 519–56.

Tefertiller, C. (1997). *Wyatt Earp: The Life Behind the Legend.* New York, NY: John Wiley and Sons.

Toronto, E. (2009). Time out of mind: dissociation in the virtual world. *Psychoanalytic Psychiatry* 26: 117–33.

Tronick, E. Z. (2001). Emotional connections and dyadic consciousness in infant—mother and patient—therapist interactions: commentary on paper by Frank M. Lachmann. *Psychoanalytic Dialogues* 11: 187–94.

Turkle, S. (1995). *Life on the Screen: Identity in the Age of the Internet.* New York, NY: Simon and Schuster.

———. (1999). Looking toward cyberspace: beyond grounded sociology. *Contemporary Sociology* 286: 643-48.

———. (2005). *The Second Self: Computers and the Human Spirit.* Cambridge, MA: MIT Press.

Tustin, F. (1986). *Autistic Barriers in Neurotic Patients.* London, UK: Karnac.

———. (1990). *The Protective Shell in Children and Adults.* London, UK: Karnac.

Tylim, I. (2010). The techno-body and the future of psychoanalysis. *Psychoanalytic Inquiry:* in press.

Valkenburg, P. M., Schouten, A. P., and Peter, J. (2005). Adolescents' identity experiments on the internet. *New Media and Society* 7: 383–402.

Valkenburg, P. M., and Peter, J. (2009). Social consequences of the Internet for adolescents: a decade of research. *Current Directions in Psychological Science:* 1–5.

Von Bertalanffy, L. (1968). *General System Theory: Foundations, Development, Applications.* New York, NY: George Braziller.

Walker, P. (2010). Muslim woman fined for wearing burqa in northern Italy. *The Guardian,* May 5, 2010. http://www.guardian.co.uk/world/2010/may/05/woman-fined-burqa-italy.

Wallace, P. (1999). *The Psychology of the Internet.* Cambridge, UK: Cambridge University Press.

Wartella, E. and Robb, M. (2008). Historical and recurring concerns about children's use of the mass media. In: *Handbook on Children and the Media.* eds. S.L. Calvert and B. Wilson, pp. 7–26. Malden, MA: Wiley-Blackwell Publishing.

Welles, J., and Wrye, H. (1991). Maternal erotic countertransference. *International Journal of Psychoanalysis* 72: 93–106.

Whang, L., Lee, S., and Chang, G. (2003). Internet over-users' psychological profiles: a behavior sampling analysis on internet addiction. *Cyberpsychological Behavior* 6: 143–50.

Wilson, T. D., Houston, C. E., and Meyers, J. M. (1998). Choose your poison: effects of lay beliefs about mental processes on attitude change. *Social Cognition* 16: 114–32.

Winnicott, D. W. (1945). Primitive emotional development. In: *Through Paediatrics to Psycho-analysis*, pp. 145–56. New York, NY: Basic Books, 1975.

———. (1953). Transitional objects and transitional phenomena. *International Journal of Psychoanalysis* 34: 89–97.

————. (1965). *The Maturational Process and the Facilitating Environment*. New York, NY: International Universities Press.

————. (1969). The use of an object. *International Journal of Psychoanalysis* 50: 711–16.

————. (1971). *Playing and Reality*. London, UK: Tavistock.

Wolf, D., and Grollman, S. H. (1982). Ways of playing: individual differences in imaginative style. In: *The Play of Children: Current Theory and Research*. eds. D.J. Pepler and K.H. Rubin, pp. 46–63. New York, NY: Karger.

Wolf, E. (1988). *Treating the Self*. New York, NY: Guilford.

World of Warfare Statistics in 2010. *MMORPG Realm*. http://www.mmorpgrealm.com/world-of-warcraft-statistic-in-2010.

Wrye, H. (1993). Erotic terror: male patients' horror of the early maternal erotic transference. *Psychoanalytic Inquiry* 13: 240–57.

Wrye, H., and Welles, J. (1994). *The Narration of Desire: Erotic Transferences and Counter-transferences*. Hillsdale, NJ: Analytic Press.

Wyatt Earp (2010). Wikipedia.com.

Yuen, C., and Lavin, M. (2004) Internet dependence in the collegiate population: the role of shyness. *Cyberpsychological Behavior* 7: 379–83.

Zhai, P. (1998). *Get Real: A Philosophical Adventure in Virtual Reality*. New York, NY: Rowman and Littlefield.

Zillmann, D., and Weaver, J. B., III. (1999). Effects of prolonged exposure to gratuitous media violence on provoked and unprovoked hostile behavior. *Journal of Applied Social Psychology* 29: 145–65.

Zizek, S. (2004). What can psychoanalysis tell us about cyberspace? *Psychoanalytic Review* 91: 801–30.

About the Editor and Contributors

Monisha C. Akhtar, Ph.D.: Faculty Member, Psychoanalytic Center of Philadelphia, Philadelphia, PA.

Salman Akhtar, M.D.: Professor of Psychiatry, Jefferson Medical College; Training and Supervising Analyst, Psychoanalytic Center of Philadelphia, Philadelphia, PA.

Jerome Blackman, M.D.: Supervising and Training Analyst, New York Freudian Society; Professor of Clinical Psychiatry at Eastern Virginia Medical School, Norfolk, VA.

Joanne Cantor, Ph.D.: Professor Emerita, Department of Communication Arts; Director, Center for Communication Research, University of Wisconsin, Madison, WI.

Frederick Fisher, M.D.: Faculty Member, Psychoanalytic Center of Philadelphia, Philadelphia, PA.

Lana Fishkin, M.D.: Faculty Member, Psychoanalytic Center of Philadelphia, Philadelphia, PA

Ralph Fishkin, D.O.: Faculty Member, Psychoanalytic Center of Philadelphia, Philadelphia, PA.

John L. Frank, M.D.: Faculty Member, Psychoanalytic Center of Philadelphia, Philadelphia, PA.

Patricia L. Gibbs, Ph.D.: Faculty Member, Michigan Psychoanalytic Institute, Dearborn, MI.

Christine C. Kieffer, Ph.D.: Faculty Member, Chicago Institute for Psychoanalysis, Chicago, IL.

Kavita I. Nayar, B.A.: Candidate in Masters Program, Broadcasting, Television, and Mass Media, Temple University, Philadelphia, PA.

Ann G. Smolen, Ph.D.: Faculty Member, Psychoanalytic Center of Philadelphia, Philadelphia, PA.

Index

academic success, media use and, 23–24
acronyms, 18; free association diversion
    through, 19
adolescent: caregiver guidance, for media
    use of, 21, 33–34, 36, 46, 70, 132;
    clinical examples of, 57–60;
    engagement, lack of, 49; group therapy
    for, 51; Internet as socially safe
    environment for, 72; male
    masturbation, with online pornography,
    60, 117; media exposure, guidance of,
    34; multitasking of, 21, 32–33, 132;
    play-acting of, 50; pornography,
    123–124; selfobject experience of, 49;
    social networking of, 51; transference
    displacement, Internet and, 89, 136
adolescent developmental phase:
    autonomy quest by, 46, 49–50, 113,
    134; Blos on, 47; chaos theory and, 45,
    48, 53; creativity in, 47; disengaging
    from family of origin during, 64;
    emergence in, 48; equifinality and, 48;
    Freud, A., on, 47; identity formation in,
    46, 47, 50–51, 64–66, 134;
    individuation in, 47, 113–114; Internet/
    text messaging and, 130; Kaplan/
    Mahler on, 47
adolescent pornography: incest and, 124;
    male masturbation and, 123–124;
    parent objection to, 124; suicide, 124

Advanced Research Projects Agency
    Network. See ARPANet
Adversarial Selfobject needs, 49
aggression. See hostility increase; media
    violence aggression
Akhtar, S., 107, 117, 138
American Academy of Pediatrics, on
    media use, 36
amygdala, 31–32, 132
anal egocentricity/narcissism, 76, 93
analyst: containment, reality/thinking/
    thought of, 79–80; countertransference
    of, 19, 73, 77, 78–79, 84, 86, 94, 120;
    cyber-language unfamiliarity of, 18; e-
    mail use by, 129
analytic method: erotic countertransference
    and, 78, 94; reality of, 78–79, 137
anonymity: cyberspace, 65; dissociative,
    66
antisocial behaviors, 28
anxiety, 29–32; separation, 90
ARPANet (Advanced Research Projects
    Agency Network), 9
asynchronicity, 66
attachment, 49, 51; child-parent, electronic
    devices and, 139; Harlow on, 62
autistic defenses, 73, 80–81, 83, 95, 122
autonomy: adolescent quest for, 46, 49–50,
    113, 134; enmeshment and, 70, 71;
    Kohut on, 49
avatar, 3, 58, 122

Bion, W. R., 60, 79, 95
"Birther" movement, Internet use in, 55
BlackBerry, 3, 14, 139
blogging, 3, 139
Blos, P., 47, 50–51
boundary: media technology influence on,
    36, 130, 138; virtual, 109
Bowlby, J., 36
Bromberg, P., 53, 134
Brown, S., 113
bullying: clinical example of, 59, 135; . *See
    also* cyberbullying
Buss-Durkee hostility inventory, 27

Cantor, J., 35, 36, 131–133, 135
CAPA. *See* Chinese American
    Psychoanalytic Alliance
caregiver, media use guidance by, 21,
    33–34, 36, 46, 70, 132; . *See also*
    helicopter parent
cell phone, 4, 46
chaos theory, 45, 48, 53
chat, 4, 10; room, 4, 84, 122; roulette, 4
child(ren): cognitive development, fear
    and, 30; development, television impact
    on, 43, 44; electronic media exposure
    of, 21; media use of, 21, 22; media
    violence aggression imitation by, 25; -
    parent attachment, 139; pornography,
    123; "real world" experiences of, 44,
    133; social networking of, 36; . *See also*
    adolescent; adolescent developmental
    phase; adolescent pornography; infant
A Child is Being Beaten (Freud, S.), 95
Chinese: Cultural Revolution, 99;
    government, CAPA support by, 110;
    pornography censorship of, 123; sexual
    drive expression inhibitions of, 117; .
    See also Skype psychoanalytic
    treatment, of Chinese
Chinese American Psychoanalytic Alliance
    (CAPA), 99, 100–101, 103, 104–105,
    106–107, 119, 137; Chinese
    government support of, 110
cognitive development: children's fear and,
    30; media technology and, 64
communication: cyberspace, 61;
    enhancement, through Internet, 1, 114
communities, 4, 135

computer, 4, 139; personal, 12;
    transference augmenting by, 97
containment, analyst, 79–80
countertransference, of analyst, 19, 73, 77,
    84, 86, 120; erotic, 78, 94; self-
    disclosure of, 78–79
creativity, 64; in adolescence
    developmental phase, 47; video game
    play curtailment of, 44
criminal violence, 24
Cultural Revolution (1966-1978), Chinese,
    99
cultural values, 45
culture, superego identification and, 116
cyberbullying, 5, 36, 59
cyber-interaction: personal identity and,
    45; social view development and, 45
cyber-language: analyst unfamiliarity with,
    18; bilingualism of, 18; free association
    and, 18; neologisms/acronyms in, 18;
    new spellings in, 18
Cyberpassion: E-Rotic Transference on the
    Internet (Gabbard), 97
cyberplay, 67–68; questions on, 67; Turkle
    on, 68
cyberselves, multiple selves and, 54–56
cybersex, 5; reality and, 84
cyberspace, 5; aggression and, 69;
    anonymity, 65; communication, 61;
    disinhibition, 65, 129; literature classics
    reformulation in, 19; psychological
    development and, 43–46; transitional
    space and, 58, 97, 135

DARPA. *See* Defense Advanced Research
    Projects Agency
Defense Advanced Research Projects
    Agency (DARPA), 9
denial of reality, 86
desensitization: "flight or fight" response
    and, 26, 31; media violence aggression
    and, 26
developmental phase, of adolescent,
    45–51, 53, 64, 64–48, 113–114, 130,
    134
developmental precursors, for thinking/
    thought, 79
developmental risks, of media use, 38

disinhibition: cyberspace and, 65, 129; Suler on, 66, 71
dissociative anonymity, 66
dissociative imagination, 67, 134
dissociative model of mind: attachment-based, 51; Bromberg on, 53; multiplicity of identity and, 51–53; Stern on, 53; Sullivan on, 53
double conscience, 51
dramatists, in play, 44
Dworkin, A., 123
dynamic therapy, 126

ego-surfer, 6
e-mail, 1, 6; analyst use of, 129; blast, 6
emergence, 48
enduring hostile mental framework, 27
engagement, adolescent lack of, 49
Engwelberg, E., 73
enmeshment, autonomy and, 70, 71
Erikson, E., 70; on play, 67–68; psychosocial development theory of, 64–65
erotic countertransference, 78, 94
erotic terror, 76, 78–79, 92, 93
escapism, virtual world and, 55
experiential mode of thought, 44
external reality, 1

Facebook, 5, 6, 14, 15, 35, 46, 51, 55, 56, 113–114, 122, 134, 135, 139
family: of origin, adolescent disengaging from, 64; time, face-to-face, 38, 39
fantasy play, 52
fantasy roles, 46
fear: amygdala influence on, 31–32, 132; children cognitive development and, 30; long-lasting, from media use, 30–31, 132; media violence and, 21, 29–32; neurophysiology of, 31, 132
female: masturbation, shame of, 117; pornography portrayal of, 123
Ferenczi, S., 51, 94, 134
Fishkin, L., Skype psychoanalytic treatment by, 115–117, 126, 137–138
Fishkin, R., Skype psychoanalytic treatment by, 118, 126, 137–138
"flight or fight" response, 26, 31

Flirting with the Virtual World (Friedman), 92
free association: acronym diversion of, 19; cyber-language and, 18
Freud, A., 47, 89
Freud, S., 1, 38, 51, 62, 67, 95, 130
Friedman, L., 92

Gabbard, G., 97
Galatzer-Levy, R. M., 49, 53, 60, 62
Gasser, U., 55, 56
gender identity disorder, 90
get naked on camera. *See* GNOC
Gibbs, P., 89, 92, 93, 94–95, 96, 97, 136–137
global village, 56
GNOC (get naked on camera), 7, 18
Google, 7, 14; stalking, 7
group therapy, for adolescent, 51

hallucinations, 87, 94
handle, 8, 13, 16
Harlow, H., 62
Heim, M., 61
helicopter parent, 8, 46, 49, 70
Hello Darkness (Brown), 113
holding environment, Winnicott on, 37
homepage, 8, 16
hostile attribution bias, 27
hostility increase: Buss-Durkee hostility inventory and, 27; enduring hostile mental framework and, 27; hostile attribution bias and, 27; interpersonal relationships and, 27; media violence and, 27–28; in movie viewing experiment, 27

identity: confusion, 46, 70; formation in adolescence, 46, 47, 50–51, 64–66, 134; gender disorder, 89; multiplicity of, 51–53, 55; personal, 45; social, 55
imagination, 139; dissociative, 67, 134; media technology and, 37–39, 44, 64, 133; video game play curtailment of, 44
IMHO (in my honest opinion), 8, 18
imitation, by infants, 28
incest, 124
individuation: in adolescence developmental phase, 47, 113–114;

separation-, 49, 90, 134
infant: imitation by, 28; research, 49
infantile symbiotic psychosis, 89
in my honest opinion. *See* IMHO
instant messaging, 8, 113, 139
internal world, Internet freer expression to, 1
Internet, 1, 9; adolescent development and, 130; as adolescent socially safe environment, 72; aggression and, 125; "Birther" movement use of, 55; communication enhancement through, 1, 114; external reality and, 1; global village need and, 56; heavy use of, by patients, 73–87; interactions, chance encounters and, 45; internal world freer expression with, 1; language of, 1–17, 18; mourning alteration of, 55; patient, heavy use of, 73–87; pornography, 122–123; sexuality/love on, 84–87; Suler on, 65, 66; transference displacement and, 89, 136; troll, 9. *See also* cyberspace
Internet addiction, 136; to "escape reality," 6.3-6.4; loneliness, 73–74; maternal erotic transference and, 76, 137; ordinary everyday psychosis, 87; personality characteristics of, 73–76, 136; to pornography, 123; projective identification and, 77–83; shyness, 73–74; South Korea rehabilitation centers for, 125
Internet Addiction Scale, 73
Interpersonalists, 52
interpersonal relationships, hostility increase and, 27
Intersubjective theorists, 49, 52
intranet, 9
invisibility, 66
iPhone, 9, 14, 113, 139
Israel, WWF viewing/playground injuries in, 25, 131

James, W., 51, 134
Janet, P., 51, 134

Kaiser Family Foundation: on media technology, 22, 23–24, 132; on media

use *vs.* academic success/contentment, 23–24
Kaplan, L., 47
Kieffer, C., 63–71, 92, 133–135
Kohlberg, L., 69
Kohut, H., 49, 124

language, of Internet, 1–17; cyber-, 18; psychosocial impact of, 18
latency, pornography and, 125
Laufer, M., 60, 94
LeDoux, J., 31, 52
Lichtenberg, J., 49
LinkedIn, 14
literature classics, cyberspace reformulation of, 19
Litowitz, Bonnie, 61
loneliness, 73–74, 130, 136
long-lasting fear, from media use, 30–31, 132

Mahler, M., 47, 49, 61, 74, 89, 134
malpractice insurance, 111
malware, 10, 16
Marcus, I., 117, 124
Margaret S. Mahler Symposium on Child Development, 41st annual, 97, 122, 129
masturbation, 81, 94; adolescent male, 123–124; female shame of, 117; with online pornography, 60, 117
maternal erotic transference, 74, 75, 136; anal egocentricity/narcissism in, 76; Internet addiction and, 76, 137
media effects, research on, 22–23
media industry, profitability/lobbying of, 23
media technology: boundaries influenced by, 36, 130, 138

Cantor on, 35; clinical examples of, 39–40; cognitive development and, 64; imagination and, 37–39, 44, 64, 133; influence of, 35–41; Kaiser Family Foundation survey on, 22, 23–24, 132; play and, 37–39, 133; psychoanalysis developmental theory and, 36–39

media use: academic success and, 23–24; caregiver guidance for, 21, 33–34, 36,

46, 70, 132; of children, 21, 22;
contentment and, 23–24; developmental
risks of, 38; effects, research on, 22–23;
long-lasting fear from, 30–31, 132;
mental health providers guidance for,
21, 33–34, 132; multitasking, of
adolescent and, 21, 32–33; negative
outcomes of, 21, 131; neurophysiology
and, 21

media violence: aggressive play and, 25,
43, 131; antisocial behaviors and, 28;
anxiety and, 29–32; Cantor on, 131;
criminal violence and, 24; fear and, 21,
29–32; hostility increase and, 27–28;
negative outcomes of, 24; repeated
exposure to, 27; sleep disturbances and,
29–32

media violence aggression, 21–29, 64, 69,
125; children imitation of, 25;
desensitization and, 26; mirror neurons
role in, 28–29, 131; social learning and,
25; WWF viewing/playground injuries
and, 25, 131

Medina, J., on multitasking, 32

mental health provider, media use
guidance of, 21, 33–34, 132

The Metaphysics of Virtual Reality
(Heim), 61

mirror neurons, 28–29, 131

Mitchell, S., 53, 134

mode of thought, narrative/experiential, 44

moral development, Kohlberg on, 69

morality, 69

Motivational Systems, of Lichtenberg, 49

mourning, Internet alteration of, 55

movie viewing, hostility increase
experiment of, 27

MUD. *See* multi-user domain

multiple selves, cyberselves and, 54–56

"Multiple Selves and Cyberselves"
(Kieffer), 134

multiplicity of identity, dissociative model
of mind and, 51–53

"Multiplicity of Identity and a Dissociative
Model of the Mind" (Kieffer), 134

multitasking, of adolescent, 132;
counterproductivity of, 32; impact of,
32–33; lower level of understanding
and, 33; media use and, 21, 32–33;

Medina on, 32; working memory
performance in, 32

multi-user domain (MUD), 55

MySpace, 5, 11, 14, 46, 51, 55, 114, 122,
134

narrative mode of thought, 44

negative outcomes: of media use, 21, 131;
from media violence, 24

neurophysiology, 131; of fear, 31, 132; on
media use, 21; mirror neurons in,
28–29, 131

object relations, 74, 84, 118

omnipotent denial, 73

online, 12; pornography, masturbation
with, 60, 117; rumors, 55

On the Influencing Machine (Tausk), 93

optimal distance, 118

ordinary everyday psychosis, 86–87, 137

Palfrey, J., 55, 56

patients, heavy Internet use and, 73–87

patterners, in play, 44

PC (personal computer), 12

PDA (Personal Digital Assistant), 12, 14

Person, E. S., 123

personal computer. *See* PC

Personal Digital Assistant. *See* PDA

personal identity, cyber-interaction and, 45

Piaget, J., 69

play: -acting, of adolescent, 50; aggressive,
media violence and, 25, 43, 131; cyber,
67–68; Erikson on nature of, 67–68;
fantasy, 52; Freud, S., on, 38, 67; media
technology and, 37–39, 133; patterners/
dramatists in, 44; Singer/Singer on, 44,
133; video game, 44; Wolf on, 44

pornography: addiction to Internet, 123;
adolescent, 123–124; child, 123;
Chinese censorship of, 123; Dworkin/
Person on, 123; female portrayal in,
123; Internet, 122–123; latency and,
125

premotor cortex, mirror neurons in, 28

preoedipal pathology, 89, 136, 137; case
examples of, 90–96

pre-oedipal transference, 74

profitability, of media industry, 23

projective identification, 73, 77–83, 93
psychoanalysis, 1; developmental theory, media technology and, 36–39; language discrepancy and, 18; literature classic reformulation and, 19; Skype treatment, 99–111; Skype treatment *vs.*, 108–109
psychological development, cyberspace and, 43–46
psychosocial: development theory, of Erikson, 64–65; impact, of Internet language, 18
Putnam, F. W., 52

rapprochement, 90
reality: analyst containment of, 79–80; of analytic method, 78–79, 137; cybersex and, 84; denial of, 86; escape, 73–74; external, 1; virtual, 62, 73, 79, 86, 94, 136
Really Simple Syndication. *See* RSS
"real world" experiences, of children, 44, 133
regression, 122
Relationalists, 51
research: infant, 49; on media effects, 22–23
Research in Motion (RIM), 3
RIM. *See* Research in Motion
RSS (Really Simple Syndication) feeds, 5, 13

sadomasochistic transference, 85–86
screen name, 13, 16
"Second Life," 4.6, 51, 55, 122
self: authorial, 52; -disclosure, 78–79; LeDoux/Putnam/Siegel on, 52; unitary, 51–53
selfobject experience, 118; of adolescent, 49; Kohut/Wolf on, 49
Self Psychologists, 49
separation anxiety, 90
separation-individuation, 49, 90, 134
sext(ing), 14, 36, 113
sexual drive, expression inhibitions, of Chinese, 117
Shengold, L., 76, 93
shyness, 73–74, 136
Siegel, D., 52
"Sim City," 4.6, 51, 55, 58, 134

Singer, D.G., 43, 44, 46, 133
Singer, J.L., 43, 44, 46, 134
single-tasking, working memory and, 33
Sjoberg, L., 73
Skorton, D., 35, 38
Skype: e-matching for dating through, 113–114; negatives for use of, 120; psychoanalytic treatment, telephone analysis *vs.*, 111; videoconferencing through, 115; videoteaching, 119
Skype psychoanalytic treatment, of Chinese, 99–111, 115–118; clinical illustrations of, 101–107; crisis in, 110; Fishkin, L., and, 115–117, 126, 137–138; Fishkin, R., and, 118, 126, 137–138; history of Chinese, 99–101; malpractice insurance for, 111; psychoanalysis *vs.*, 108–109; questions on, 108–111; in repressive political regime, 110–111; security of, 109; telephone analysis *vs.*, 111; virtual boundary in, 109
sleep disturbances, media violence and, 29–32
smartphones, 14, 35, 46
Snyder, E., 99, 137
social-emotional learning, 44
social identity, social networking and, 55
social learning, media violence aggression and, 25
social media, 14; Facebook, 5, 6, 14, 15, 35, 46, 51, 55, 56, 113–114, 122, 134, 135, 139; LinkedIn, 14; MySpace, 5, 11, 14, 46, 51, 55, 114, 122, 134; Twitter, 13, 14, 15, 35
social networking, 14; of adolescent, 51; children and, 36; Palfrey/Gasser on, 56; social identity and, 55
social networking sites. *See* social media
social values, 45
solipsistic introjection, 66
South Korea, Internet addiction rehabilitation centers of, 125
Stages in the Development of the Sense of Reality (Ferenczi), 94
Stern, D., 53
Stoller, R. J., 90, 94
suicide, 35; adolescent, 124

Suler, J., 65; on disinhibition, 66, 71; on
  Internet behavior/group process, 65, 66
Sullivan, H. S., 53, 134
superego identification, 130; culture and,
  116; regression of, 122
symbiotic phase of development, 89–90

Tausk, V., 93
telephone analysis, Skype psychoanalytic
  treatment *vs.*, 111
television, child development impact of,
  43, 44
text messaging, 15, 17, 56, 113, 139;
  adolescent development and, 130
thought: analyst containment of, 79–80;
  developmental precursors for, 79;
  narrative/experiental mode of, 44
transference, 73, 84, 86, 95, 103, 104;
  computer augmenting, 97;
  displacement, Internet and, 89, 136;
  maternal erotic, 74, 75, 76, 136, 137;
  pre-oedipal, 74; sadomasochistic,
  85–86; . *See also* countertransference
transitional space, 50, 53, 70; cyberspace
  and, 58, 97, 135; of virtual world, 56;
  Winnicott on, 37
Turkle, S.-33, 45, 54, 68, 72, 134
Twitter, 13, 14, 15, 35

unconscious defenses, 119
understanding, lower level of, multitasking
  and, 33
unformulated experience, 53

UR (you are), 18, 19
username, 13, 16

verbalization, 93
video game play, imaginative play/
  creativity curtailed by, 44
violence. *See* hostility increase; media
  violence; media violence aggression
virtual boundary, 109
virtual reality, 86, 94, 136; patient
  preference for, 73; reality and, 62, 79
virtual worlds: multiple identity and,
  51–53, 55; transitional space of, 56

Welles, J., 74, 76, 79, 92
"Why Men have Extramarital Affairs"
  (Akhtar), 117
widget, 5, 10, 17
Winnicott, D., 37, 50
Wolf, E., 44, 49
working memory: multitasking and, 32;
  single-tasking and, 33
World of Warcraft Internet game, 125
World Wrestling Federation (WWF),
  viewing/playground injuries, in Israel
  and, 25, 131
Wrye, H., 74, 76, 79, 92

you are. *See* UR
YouTube, 5, 17, 63, 69

Zizek, S., 62, 84